CW00607367

ELEPHANT MIDWIVES, PARROT DUETS

ELEPHANT MIDWIVES, PARROT DUETS

AND OTHER INTRIGUING FACTS FROM THE ANIMAL KINGDOM

WARREN D. THOMAS
AND DANIEL KAUFMAN

illustrations by Mallory Pearce

Robson Books

First published in Great Britain in 1991
by Robson Books Ltd, Bolsover House,
5-6 Clipstone Street, London W1P 7EB

Copyright © 1990 Daniel Kaufman
The right of Warren D Thomas and Daniel
Kaufman to be identified as author of this
work has been asserted by them in accordance
with the Copyright, Designs and Patents
Act 1988

Design by Susan Shankin

British Library Cataloguing in Publication Data
Thomas, Warren D.
  Elephant midwives, parrot duets and other
  intriguing facts from the animal kingdom.
  I. Title II. Kaufman, Daniel
  591

  ISBN 086051 747 0

Printed in Great Britain by
Billing & Sons Ltd, Worcester

Daniel Kaufman wishes to dedicate this book to all his favorite animal-lovers, including especially his wife, Gina; her mother, Jackie Ficarotta; and St. Francis, Denise Cabral, Mary Beth Crain, Terry Taylor, and Francis Jeffrey.

Daniel also dedicates this book to his beloved spritely cats, Burp and Yogi.

CONTENTS

INTRODUCTION ix

PART 1 A WORLD FULL
OF ANIMALS 1
Animal Evolution 3
Animal Numbers 17
Animal Bodies and Senses 31

PART 2 GETTING ALONG IN THE
ANIMAL KINGDOM 69
Animals Cooperating 71
Animals Communicating 81
Animal Communities 103

PART 3 HUNTING AND HIDING 115
Animals Surviving 117
Animal Predators 129

PART 4 MAKING MORE ANIMALS 145
Animals Courting 147
Animals Caring 167

ACKNOWLEDGMENTS

Daniel Kaufman gratefully acknowledges his friend Marty Elkort, whose oft-inspired writing graces many of the astonishing facts in this book.

He also wishes to acknowledge the generous and helpful assistance of Donna Zerner, and Ralph Helfer.

Sources for the information in this book are too numerous to list, but of those we personally spoke with, we wish to acknowledge the helpful suggestions of Mike Crotty, Doug Thompson, and Francis Jeffrey.

We would also like to thank Jeremy Tarcher for his idea to write this book, for the inspiration he has provided, and for his patience in helping to make this book one we may all be proud of.

Last, and perhaps most indispensable, Jeremy Tarcher's dedicated editor Daniel Malvin deserves a round of applause and perhaps a standing ovation for his superb editorial feedback and support.

INTRODUCTION

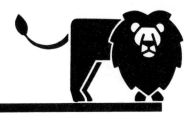

For almost 4 billion years the laboratory of nature has been experimenting with an immense diversity of animal species. Billions of extraordinary and exquisitely evolved creatures share our planet with us. Yet over the course of only a few centuries humans have brought thousands of species to extinction or near-extinction.

The world loses up to three animal species per day, and some scientists predict that just ten years from now the rate will increase to three species extinctions per hour. We are destroying the crucial pieces of the fabric holding entire ecosystems together. As humans continue to consume the last remaining tracts of habitable land, the world faces the extinction of half its animal species within the next several decades.

In the past twenty-five years nearly half of the Amazon rain forests have been sold to oil and lumber companies for commercial purposes. As their trees are converted into lumber and the land cleared for agriculture, ecosystems that took millennia to develop are being thrown totally out of balance within a few short months.

Once there were several hundred thousand blue whales swimming in the world's oceans; today fewer than 1,500 remain. In the 1970s and '80s over half a million dolphins were unnecessarily killed by fishermen who set their nets to catch tuna. Once there were hundreds of thousands of elephants roaming the earth; in a few short years humans have reduced these herds to a few thousand.

In the great kingdom of animals, human beings are certainly king. For a good king to reign wisely he must learn to appreciate and to love his subjects, to see how their lives give value to his own. From the plant and animal kingdoms we learn new concepts and new ways of treating disease, and above all we learn to appreciate the wonder of life itself. Now is the time for all human beings to recognize the importance of each and every fellow creature on the planet we share.

Every existing plant or animal species may hold a clue to a potential remedy, cure, or treatment for a human ailment. We too easily forget the gifts from plants and animals that nourish and sustain our lives, and there are gifts we are only now learning about that may revolutionize the treatment of cancer and a host of other ills. The liver of sharks, for example, appears to contain a substance called catrex, which has powerful antitumor effects. Even the lowly bacteria and viruses have taught us lessons that scientists have used to create new medications and vaccines. The shark has existed on earth for 400 million years and dolphins for 40 million years, whereas humans have existed for only 400,000 years. We have much indeed to learn from our animal neighbors.

For centuries the healing effects of certain animals on both the mentally and physically ill have been appreciated. The love of a pet cat, dog, rabbit, or canary can give voice to a speechless autistic child. Many older people live their lives for the love of a pet that has never betrayed or abandoned them. It is no wonder that Bast, the 3,000-year-old

Egyptian cat goddess, was one of the great healing deities of the ancient world.

Animal fables have been used by the greatest writers and within the most sacred works of literature since the beginning of recorded history. Generation upon generation of spiritual seekers have learned important lessons from the animal stories that abound in holy books. The basis of Hindu mythology begins with the Pancha Tantra, a ten-thousand-year-old Sanskrit text almost entirely about animals.

A deepening appreciation of what we learn from animals, in addition to our awe and wonder at the magic of the animal kingdom, may lead us back to the respect and reverence we as a species once held for the creatures of the earth before civilization began to threaten the existence of millions of our animal neighbors.

Think of this book as a love song. We must practice love on animals. Human beings are not separate from animals, nor are they better than nor older than animals. We are a different kind of animal, one that can know itself with the awareness that it does so. This self-awareness is our ticket to love, and that love must extend to the non-human life on this planet, which is crying out for attention, for healing and for respect.

ONE

A World Full of Animals

ANIMAL EVOLUTION

MYSTERIES OF EVOLUTION

The animal kingdom is filled with hints of the dim evolutionary past. Like the footprints of dinosaurs long gone, the clues are there to be discovered.

The crocodile indeed is a living relic, a survivor through time from the age of giants. The horseshoe crab is unchanged from his ancestors who swam along the beaches 300 million years ago. Why did this creature not evolve into something else, or become extinct, as did other animals of that time? The wings of the penguin, which once allowed it to fly, evolved into reliable flippers that propel him through the water with ease. Whales have hind legs in the womb that disappear before birth. Once, whales shook the trees as they thudded heavily through the swamps. The baleen whales have no teeth, and they feed by filtering water to sift out the microscopic plankton. Yet in the womb

3

it has a set of teeth. Like the whale's phantom hind legs, these teeth disappear before birth. Marsupial mammals have vestiges of a tooth once used to break out of eggs, something they have not done for 75 million years.

Female porposies have eight teats while in the womb but only two when they are born. Millions of years ago porpoises investigated rivers in India, chasing fish upstream. They liked what they found and settled in the muddy, dark streams. Today, the river porpoise of India is blind, its vestigial eyes shrunk to pinhole size and able only to discern dark from light. It senses its environment not by sight but by ultrasound, a form of echolocation using sound pulses that emanate from the porpoise's head.

The fossil record can be made sense of by accepting the idea that certain animals gave rise to new and different animals during the course of geologic time. This process is what we call evolution. Animals with bones or shells have left behind the best fossils, while the traces of soft-bodied animals are very rare in the fossil record. Despite the gaps in the record, a rather complete picture of the development of life on earth has been deduced through careful study of the fossil clues discovered in rocks from around the world. The following chronology points out some of the important highlights in the development of animal life on Earth.

The Origin of the Earth

Roughly 4.6 billion years ago the planet earth was formed from a collection of lifeless gases, dust, and rocks. All of the elements necessary for the future development of life were added to the planet's inventory. The primordial atmosphere was dominated by nitrogen gas and carbon dioxide.

Oxygen

Traces of single-celled organisms resembling algae have been found in rocks dating back 3.5 billion years. By 2,200 million years ago blue-green algae were common on earth and through photosynthesis they introduced oxygen into the atmosphere, leading to an environment more hospitable to the development of new forms of life.

Multicelled Animals

By 700 million years ago, small invertebrate animals lived on the ocean floor, leaving tracks, burrows, and other traces of their activities. Jellyfish and soft-bodied corals called sea-pens dwell in the oceans along with a vast variety of segmented worms.

The Explosion of Life

A great diversification of life occurred in the oceans about 590 million years ago. Because of the evolution of shells and other hard body parts, which have been well preserved, this period marks the first appearance of abundant fossils. Sponges, primitive mollusks, including relatives of the modern-day *Nautilus*, and the ancestors of starfish and sea urchins were common.

The First Vertebrates

By 500 million years before the present day the first true vertebrates, the jawless fishes, prowled the water. Lampreys and hagfishes, although much changed from their ancestors, are modern representatives of these early jawless fishes. The diversity of mollusks continued to increase.

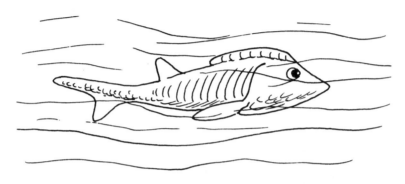

The First Jawed Fishes

The first fish with true jaws became the dominant predators in the water about 460 million years ago. These fish probably evolved in fresh water, not in the ocean. The first land plants made headway in the generally warm climate of the time.

The Age of Fishes

An immense variety of bony fish appeared about 400 million years ago and went on to populate the world's oceans. Sharks and skates, having skeletons composed entirely of cartilage, made their appearance during this same time period. Amphibians began to evolve from one line of bony fishes and became the first vertebrate animals to venture onto land.

The First Reptiles

The first reptiles evolved from primitive amphibians about 300 million years ago. While amphibians must return to the water in order to lay their eggs, the life cycle of reptiles is liberated from the water by the development of the amniotic egg with its tough shell protecting the developing young. The first insects also appeared in the fossil record at about this time. The largest flying insect ever, which looked like a modern dragonfly but had a wingspan of over 2 feet, left traces of its life 300 million years ago. Cockroaches made their first appearance on the scene at about this time.

Mass Extinction

A cataclysmic extinction episode about 230 million years ago erased from earth fully 90 percent of marine invertebrate species and ushered in a new period of life. The extinctions coincided with the joining together all of earth's land masses into a huge supercontinent called Pangaea. Many shallow seas dried up and disappeared, and the formation of Pangaea brought into competitive contact many animals that previously had been separated.

The Age of Reptiles began in earnest, and the earliest dinosaurs appeared on earth. The first mammals appeared, descendants from one line of reptiles.

The Age of Dinosaurs

By 200 million years ago the supercontinent of Pangaea had divided into two separate main land masses. Dinosaurs increased in diversity and dominance. The first bird yet uncovered, *Archaeopteryx*, which had many body features indicating its close relation to reptiles, lived 160 million years ago.

The First Snakes

It was roughly 140 million years ago that snakes first appeared. Sometime around 135 million years ago the marsupials and the earliest forms of placental mammals became diversified and begin to find their niches. During this period *Hesperornis*, a sea bird without wings, swam the oceans, using its oversized back feet for propulsion.

The Age of Mammals

At 65 million years before the present, the Age of the Dinosaurs officially ended with a great extinction of life that eliminated most reptile species. Only turtles, snakes, lizards, and crocodiles survived to represent reptiles in later ages. The Age of Mammals began in earnest with an explosive diversification of animals, and the first rodents began to populate the earth. Tree-dwelling lemurs appeared on the scene as the first primates, setting the stage for the future descent of apes and monkeys.

Mammals Diversify

Eohippus, the earliest member of the line of animals leading to the horse, roamed parts of North America about 50 million years ago. About the size of a house cat, *Eohippus* had four toes on its front feet and three on its hind feet. The earliest fossils of monkeys and apes could be found in rocks deposited 40 million years ago. The first whales, as well as the first bats, lived during this time.

In North Africa early elephants roamed the plains about 30 million years ago. Camels could be found in North America, but later they would migrate to Asia and they eventually disappeared from North America. The llamas and vicunas of South America are descended from the early camels of North America. Around 15 million years ago a 10-foot-tall flightless bird named *Phororhacos*, with a huge hooked beak, lived in South America.

The Rise of Humans

By 10 million years ago antelopes and giraffes were common on the plains of Africa. The hippopotamus appeared on the scene for the first time. Pigs and deer dominated Europe and Asia, and bears and true cats had become common. By about 2 million years ago true dogs, such as the wolves, were the dominant meat-eating animals in the northern hemisphere.

Early man, *Homo erectus*, appeared on the scene about 1.5 million years ago, living in small tribes. It wasn't until about 130,000 years ago that Neanderthal man emerged as a versatile tool-using creature. Cro-Magnons, regarded as modern humans, appeared about 40,000 years ago.

RELICS
AND
RARITIES

The Monster Who Rose from the Dead

By careful examination of fossilized remains, scientists concluded that the coelacanth, a fish closely related to the ancestors of the first land-dwelling amphibians, died out 70 million years ago along with dinosaurs and other creatures from the dim past. Imagine the surprise when in 1938 a very-much-alive coelacanth was caught by native fishermen off the coast of South Africa!

This "living fossil" was 5 feet long, dark blue, and weighed 127 pounds. It had a thick vertical tail and four large fleshy fins that led to its nickname, "old four legs." Since its first discovery, other coelacanths have been caught, mostly in the Indian Ocean.

An Evolutionary Oddity

The island of Madagascar is the home of many strange animal species, the most astonishing of which is the bushy-tailed little aye-aye. When first observed in 1780 by a French explorer, the aye-aye appeared to be a rodent, with the rat's characteristic teeth—perhaps a new species of squirrel. But upon closer anatomical examination, scientists decided to reclassify it as a distant relative of monkeys and human beings, in part because it possesses an opposable thumb, a characteristic of primates.

Hidden deep in the mangrove swamps of Madagascar in retreat from encroaching civilization, the aye-aye are nocturnal creatures who sleep by day atop tall trees and are seldom visible. An occasional screeching cry "like the sound of two pieces of metal scraped together" is the only sign of this mysterious creature with a face like a cat's and the body of a squirrel-monkey.

The aye-aye lives off the grubs and larvae it finds beneath tree bark. The long middle finger and clasping thumb enable it to creep so silently along a branch that it can hear the telltale sound of a grub chewing. If the aye-aye fails to detect any grubs present, it delicately taps along the branch with its long middle finger until it hears a hollow rap indicating the presence of a bore-hole underneath. In seconds it strips away the bark and hooks its finger into any available hole to grab the grub.

The aye-aye is an evolutionary oddity because it is the sole survivor of a small group of species—perhaps even a single animal—that has managed to preserve its own solitary line of evolutionary descent for millions of years, an exceptionally rare occurrence in the animal kingdom.

Looking Up

The Tuatara is the sole survivor of a group of primitive reptiles that otherwise became extinct 100 million years ago. The few remaining Tuatara live in remote areas of New Zealand, where they are protected by the government. The lizardlike animal may be up to 25 inches long and is extremely slow-growing. It incubates eggs for up to 425 days, compared to forty-two days for a typical grass lizard or sixty-one for an alligator.

The Tuatara is of particular interest to biologists because of its numerous primitive features, which are nearly identical to features found in fossils, including a well-developed parietal "eye," complete with traces of a rudimentary retina and a lens, located on the top of its head. This third eye is akin to a skylight. It is covered with scales and probably does not have a modern-day function, but it may have been an important sense organ in early reptiles.

Missing Links?

At first they thought it was a hoax. Some joker had pasted the beak of a duck on a beaver skin, and now they were trying to fob the result off as a real animal. Derision gave way to amazement in nineteenth-century England when the truth came out. The duck-billed platypus is not a joke, but rather a primitive mammal called a monotreme that lays eggs and also nurses its young. It has a leathery beak instead of a normal mammalian mouth. The platypus spends much of its life in the water, hunting at night. It can stay underwater without breathing for ten minutes at a time, with its eyes, ears, and nostrils closed, storing its catch in cheek pouches until it emerges. The platypus may eat half its weight in food every night.

The spiny anteater, also called the echidna, of Australia is the only other living monotreme. It has a pouch that opens only during the mating season. The echidna lays one egg, with a soft, pliable skin, and places it in its pouch to incubate. When the baby echidna is born (the mother breaks the shell with her snout to get the baby out), it feeds on mother's milk, but not in the normal way. Monotremes lack nipples, and so the mother echidna lies on her back and the milk oozes through her skin from pores in her belly to be lapped up by the babies, who increase their weight 100-fold in the first three weeks in their mother's pouch. The echidna also has the lowest blood temperature of any mammal, around 75 degrees Fahrenheit. It has spines like a porcupine and, when threatened, curls up in a protective ball. Its front feet face forward and its rear feet outward, giving the animal a waddling gait. The echidna feasts on ants and termites that it digs out of the ground with its long claws and ingests with a long, slender tongue.

The living monotremes, the duck-billed platypus and the echidna, are representatives of the first true mammals to appear on earth and thus are one of the missing links between reptiles and mammals.

Snakes at Sea
The sea snakes of the Pacific and Indian oceans reverted from land to the sea and readapted for an aquatic life. Their elongated lung (most snakes have only one lung; the other disappeared long ago) serves as a storage bag for air and

also as an internal flotation device. Their tail is flattened and is used as a paddle, and their nostrils close tightly in the water. All snakes can swim gracefully and speedily, moving even more easily in water than on land, but the sea snakes—all of which are poisonous—have developed to live full time in their watery home.

Topsy-Turvy
In the Nile River of Egypt lives the Nile catfish, a fish that swims upside down. The belly of this odd fish is colored gray, and the back, facing down, is white. How this fish came to the conclusion that up is down is a mystery, as is the benefit that this strange swimming orientation confers on the catfish. The ancient Egyptians, who had a liking for such novelties, made statues and paintings of this upside-down wonder.

Pockets of Evolution
Marsupials are odd mammals in that they raise and carry their young around in pockets. Most of the world's marsupials live in Australia, where they have been protected by isolation from the dominance of the placental mammals who prevail everywhere else.

Placental mammals carry their young for longer periods, giving birth to animals that are far along developmentally; some require only a short period of protection before venturing into the world. Marsupials have a short gestation, giving birth to offspring that need a longer period of development outside the womb before becoming self-sufficient. The red kangaroo, just under six feet tall and weighing two hundred pounds, takes only five weeks from conception to birth, producing blind offspring less than an inch long, hairless and helpless as it climbs towards the safety of its mother's pouch.

When the Going Gets Tough

Since the Ice Age, little pupfish have lived in the scattered water holes of Death Valley, one of the harshest environments on earth. They survive equally well in fresh water and in the many salt-water pools of the area, where the salinity may be close to that of the ocean. The pupfish can survive temperatures from 38 to 108 degrees Fahrenheit and can even last a few minutes at 111 degrees.

The Long Sleep

In the Australian desert there is a frog that lies dormant underground for eleven months of the year. During the brief rainy season it comes out of the ground and fills up its body with water, gorges itself with food, and lays its eggs. Then the frog returns to a burrow underground and waits passively in a state of suspended animation for eleven more months.

The Longest Sleep

The tardigrade, a microscopic creature, is also called the water bear, because it resembles a miniature bear with many legs. Tardigrades live in moss, and when the moss dries out this tiny creature goes into a state of profound dormancy. When in this state of suspended animation, a tardigrade can survive temperatures from 308 degrees Fahrenheit to an incredible minus 459 degrees. In one celebrated instance, some dried moss that had lain on a shelf in a museum for 120 years was placed in water, and soon several tardigrades were reanimated and moving about.

ANIMAL NUMBERS

By some estimates there are over 10^{33} (10 followed by 33 zeros) animals living on earth, representing more than a million separate animal species, and life scientists are adding a thousand or more species to the list each year. A species is a group of interbreeding individuals of common ancestry that are reproductively isolated from all other such groups. Human beings certainly have a lot to be proud of, but with just over 5.3 billion members, *Homo sapiens* really is just a small player in the grand web of animal life.

There are more than 800,000 species of insects; 21,000 species of fish; 2,500 species of amphibians; 7,000 species of reptiles; 9,000 species of birds; and, finally, 4,500 species of mammals.

Counting Off
The United States has the most cats of any nation, about 40 million. There are believed to be as many chickens in the world as there are people. The world's horse population is currently estimated to be about 90 million. There

are fifteen times as many raccoons living in cities as there are in the woods. There are over one quadrillion ants living on the earth at any given time.

It Is Written

When the great clock of life was wound up, all mammals received the same amount of heartbeats to use during their lifetimes: 800,000,000. The rate at which the beats are used roughly determines how long a certain mammal will live. The elephant's great heart pulses thirty times a minute, and at that rate it takes the average elephant over fifty years to use its allotment. If you think your meter is ticking too fast, relax. Somehow, human beings are exempted from the rule: Scientists believe the size of the brain prevails over the rationing of heartbeats.

Life Is Short

The pygmy shrew is one of the world's smallest mammals. The adult may weigh as little as one-twentieth of an ounce and measure between 1½ and 2 inches from its snout to the base of its 1-inch tail. This tiny predator can be found along the northern coast of the Mediterranean Sea. It has very poor eyesight, and its sense of smell is effective only at fairly short range. The pygmy shrew's heart is twice as large as other mammals' in proportion to its body dimensions, and it pumps at a rate of 900 to 1,400 beats per minute. The shrew has the highest metabolic rate of any mammal, and its lifespan is a scant 1½ years. Simply in order to live at such a rapid pace, it must consume the equivalent of twice its body weight every day.

The Effect of Captivity on Longevity

Some animals are known to live much longer than average in captivity, some much shorter. It is difficult to estimate the natural maximum lifespan for many animals, because they have never been thoroughly studied in their native habitat. Based on studies of captive animals, the following table lists a few of the maximum lifespans found in the animal kingdom.

Animal	Maximum Lifespan in Years
Tortoise	138
Whale	95
Salamander	80
Elephant	78
Condor	72
Hippopotamus	51
Horse	46
Boa constrictor	40
Dolphin	35
Cat	34
Giraffe	30
Brown bear	30
Seal	25
Leopard	24
Jaguar	22
Platypus	17
Kangaroo	16
Sheep	15
Koala	12
Porcupine	10
Opossum	8
Mouse	3

High Jumpers and Broad Jumpers

The most astonishing jumper in the animal kingdom is the klipspringer, a small antelope found in many mountainous areas of Africa. Klipspringers are well known for their ability to scramble up nearly vertical cliffs, using very small projections on the cliff face as footholds. Vertical jumps of 25 to 30 feet are not uncommon for this leaping antelope. The figures in the following table do not represent the maximum possible jump for the species concerned, but rather the approximate distances that a number of animals have been known to jump.

Animal	Horizontal (feet)	Vertical (feet)
Impala	40	
Horse	37	
Kangaroo	30	9
Jack rabbit	25	
Elk		10
Deer		10
Leopard		10
Lion	6	

Animal Speeds

The fastest animal on the ground probably is the cheetah, which can deliver explosive bursts of speed of nearly 70 miles per hour over short distances. The cheetah uses its tail as a rudder in the wind while running at top speeds. One of the slowest animals, the snail, clocks in at 0.03 miles per hour. A tortoise, at 0.17 miles per hour, can easily out-walk a snail.

Animal	Maximum Speed (miles per hour)
Cheetah	65+
Pronghorn	65+
Lion, horse, ostrich	50
Jack rabbit, coyote	45
Greyhound	40
Bear	35
Cat	30
Rhinoceros	28
Elephant	25
Wild turkey	15
Black mamba snake	12
Pig	11
Chicken	9
Sloth	.15

The Fastest Fish

In general, the larger the fish, the faster it can swim. A 24-inch salmon can sprint at 14 miles per hour, and a 48-inch barracuda is capable of reaching a top speed of about 27 miles per hour. The fastest animal underwater is the cosmopolitan sailfish, who has been clocked at a speed of 68 miles per hour, covering a distance of one hundred yards in just three seconds. Swordfish and marlin are thought to be capable of similarly incredible bursts of speed. No fish can swim at top speed for more than a brief time, and normal cruising speeds are much lower.

Flying Feats

The aptly named "swift" cruises high above the meadows of England at 60 miles per hour. Its great speed enables it to outrace its enemies and feed with little trouble, scooping spiders and insects from the air as it soars along. Without ever alighting, the swift bathes by flying into rainstorms or dive bombing ponds and streams. It gathers airborne material for the nest and is the only bird to copulate in midair. To top it off, the swift flies to South Africa every year, a distance of many thousands of miles. One of the fastest birds, the sandpiper has been clocked at 110 miles per hour, easily leaving behind the airplane observing them.

The albatross, with its twelve-foot wingspan, can glide for six days without beating its wings and can even sleep in midair while gliding at speeds of 19 to 35 miles per hour. Bar-headed geese have been observed at 29,000 feet, flying over the top of Mount Everest.

The tiny hummingbird can fly at speeds greater than 50 miles per hour, can beat its wings more than 60 times per second, and is the only bird that can fly backwards. It is a creature of the New World, and there are no native hummingbirds in Europe or Asia.

Flying Fish

The common flying fish measures 7 to 10 inches in length and is found in tropical and equatorial waters. When the flying fish is pursued, it angles upward through the water and vibrates its tail fin very rapidly until its body is lifted entirely out of the water. The flying fish extends its highly developed pectoral fins and begins to skim over the water at a height of 6 to 10 feet. In just a few seconds it can cover a distance of 50 yards, and with a tailwind can glide as far as 200 yards. It does not actually flap its fins, but keeps them in a fixed position while it glides through the air.

The Fastest Animal Motion

The fastest physical action yet recorded of any animal is the wing-beat of the common midge. This tiny insect normally beats its wings 57,000 times per minute, but it is capable of increasing that speed to a rate of 133,000 times per minute. This is equivalent to a camera shutter speed of $\frac{1}{2,218}$ second.

The Largest on Land

Elephant statistics are as colossal as a circus poster. An African bull weighs up to seven tons and measures as high as eleven feet at the shoulder. Elephants have one of the biggest and least-efficient digestive systems of any animal. In order to compensate for the inefficiency, the elephant will eat up to 500 pounds of foliage a day.

A female African elephant must endure twenty-one months from impregnation to birth if the calf is a male. Tusks can weigh up to 225 pounds; their record length is eleven feet, six inches. Despite their great weight and the racket they can make, elephants can glide silently through the jungle if they wish. The elephant has only two enemies.

One is the tiger, whose depredations are controllable. The deadlier enemy, about to drive elephants into extinction, is the creature the elephant has served well throughout history but that now has less need for his services: humans.

The Largest on Earth

The largest animal inhabitant of the earth is the blue whale, weighing in at eighty tons (160,000 pounds) and measuring over 100 feet in length. The blue whale is the largest animal that has ever lived on the earth, including dinosaurs. The largest known dinosaur skeleton measures 88 feet long, and the heaviest estimated weight of a dinosaur is fifty tons. The tongue of the largest blue whale is bigger than an automobile, its blood supply exceeds 15,000 pints, and its weight exceeds that of twenty-four elephants. Protected by a layer of fat or blubber up to two feet thick, some whales can dive to depths as great as 3,200 feet. This was discovered in 1932 when a blundering sperm whale became entangled in a cable on the ocean floor.

Small Ones

The smallest fish known is the Marshall Islands goby, which measures less than half an inch in length. The smallest known reptile can be found in a species of the gecko. An adult gecko of the species *Sphaerodactylus parthenopion* measures only three-quarters of an inch from the tip of its nose to the base of its tail. The smallest bird in the world is Helena's or bee hummingbird from Cuba. An average adult measures only 2¼ inches from bill tip to tail.

How Much Do They Weigh?

Animal	Average weight
Sperm whale	74,000 pounds
African elephant	14,000 pounds
Walrus	3,200 pounds
Cow	1,800 pounds
Moose	800 pounds
Polar bear	715 pounds
Llama	375 pounds
Mountain lion	170 pounds
Cheetah	128 pounds
Porpoise	103 pounds
Coyote	75 pounds
Beaver	59 pounds
Porcupine	28 pounds
Raccoon	21 pounds
Otter	13 pounds
Chicken	7 pounds
Rat	1 pound
Gerbil	4.4 ounces
Pygmy shrew	0.16 ounce
Helena's hummingbird	0.07 ounce

Some Facts About Snakes

Snakes are among the most feared creatures on earth, yet there remains a vast ignorance about these beautiful animals. Here are some facts: Of the approximately 2,500 species existing, about 600 are poisonous. Of these, only about 150 are capable of killing humans with their venom. The viper family has the most elaborate apparatus: retractable fangs that lie flat when not in use and spring erect when needed. Backed by ducts connected to sacs or reservoirs containing poison, they pump venom through hollow fangs, injecting it efficiently into the hapless victim. Cobra and mamba venom works on the nerves, causing paralysis and heart stoppage; rattlesnake and viper venom attacks the blood, causing hemorrhaging and shock. The biggest of the venomous snakes is the king cobra, which can grow to a length of more than 18 feet. Snakes, like all reptiles, continue to grow throughout their lives.

Australia has some of the world's deadliest snakes, such as the death adder, which kills 50 percent of humans it bites, and the tiger snake, which kills about 25 percent. The enormous taipan of Australia produces 30 percent more venom than the tiger snake and is considered the most dangerous of the reptiles.

Although most snakes live on the ground, the deadly green mamba of Africa waits unseen on a tree branch and simply drops down onto a passing victim. The golden tree snake of India is able to glide through the air for distances up to 150 feet by flattening its body into a more aerodynamic shape.

The largest snakes are the nonpoisonous boas and pythons, who kill by constricting or squeezing their victim until it dies of suffocation. The record length for an anaconda is 29 feet, with a weight of over 300 pounds. Pythons and constrictors are said to eat anything they can swallow from a mouse to a small cow to fully grown kangaroos in Australia.

Clock Rhythms

Every living thing is governed by some sort of timer, and most animals live by the twenty-four-hour day. Many animals spend the daylight hours hunting for food and sleep at night. In contrast, nocturnal animals, such as owls, are most active during the night. Yet it does not seem that sunlight is the most important component in telling an animal what time it is. Scientists have in recent years been able to demonstrate that for birds and reptiles the sense of time is governed by the small pineal gland in the brain. In mammals the master timekeeper appears to be located in a small cluster of cells in the hypothalamus area of the brain, called the suprachiasmatic nucleus.

Slow Motion

If a snail gets tapped on its head, it will curl up inside its shell and hide until the danger passes. The same snail, however, if tapped on the head at a rate of four or more beats per second, will not perceive the taps and will move along as though nothing is amiss.

Hitting the Sack

There really is no agreement among scientists as to the essential nature of sleep. For some animals it may be a means of conserving body energy, since the body's metabolism slows down during sleep. Many animals are careful to find a secure place in which to sleep, whereby their sleeping may help them avoid predators.

There is a great range in the amount of time that various animals spend sleeping. Based on studies of animals held in captivity, the following table lists the total sleep time per twenty-four hours for a variety of mammals.

Hours of Sleep	Animal
22	Koala
20	Two-toed sloth
19	Armadillo, oppossum
16	Lemur
14	Hamster, squirrel
13	Rat, cat, pig
12	Spiny anteater
11	Jaguar
10	Chimpanzee, rabbit
8	Man, mole
7	Cow
6	Sheep
5	Horse, bottlenose dolphin
4	Giraffe, elephant
0	Shrew

Sound Sleepers

During the cold winter months, when food is scarce, many small mammals enter a prolonged and controlled state of dormancy known as hibernation. True hibernators, such as ground squirrels, marmots, and woodchucks, prepare for hibernation by building up large amounts of body fat. During hibernation the animal's body temperature cools to within a degree or so of the ambient temperature and its metabolism slows down dramatically. In the ground squirrel the respiration rate decreases from a norm of 200 breaths per minute to around five per minute, and the heart rate decreases from 150 to five beats per minute.

Some mammals, such as bears and raccoons, enter a state of prolonged sleep in winter but with little or no decrease in body temperature. This is not true hibernation, and these animals can be awakened quite easily.

ANIMAL
BODIES AND SENSES

In order to assure that animals will survive in the extreme range of climates and terrains on land and in the sea, nature has experimented with an extraordinary variety of features in the design of animal bodies and animal senses. Fishes can see in the blackest depths with the aid of light from bioluminescent bacteria in their bodies; bats can navigate in the pitch black of caves; whales can hear their brethren warning of danger thousands of miles distant; dogs can smell even the minutest traces of a scent in the air or on the ground. On and on the bodies and senses of animals bear witness to the success of nature's progressive accomplishments. The variety of effective sensory apparatus seems nearly endless, but despite the immense diversity to be found in the animal kingdom's organs of perception nature's basic principles remain discernible: senses are for survival, and most forms serve a function.

Animals in their special ways are millions of years ahead of the best human engineers in the development of special body plans and senses to help them to reproduce, navigate, and find food and to protect them from enemies. The specialized abilities of many animals are a wonder to behold and can teach us much about how nature solves some of the most insurmountable problems one can imagine.

A Floating Organizational Chart

The Portuguese man-of-war jellyfish is not one single creature but a corporation: many individuals working together, each in charge of a different department. It is a floating organizational chart, a community of interests with the same bottom-line goal: survival. A deceptively pretty blue-and-pink airbag that doubles as a sail keeps the enterprise afloat. Tentacles hanging down 45 feet await the arrival of unsuspecting fish. The tentacles wrap around a victim, stinging it to death, then draw the body up into the creature's stomach. Most jellyfish merely sting. The Portuguese man-of-war does more than sting: its deadly venom can kill a human being. All tentacles are not involved in catching food; each is a separate animal with differing responsibilities to the corporate body. Some are devoted to reproduction, some to offense, others to defense, while others keep the man-of-war balanced.

This seagoing enterprise has one employee, *nomeus*, a janitor fish that keeps the jellyfish's tentacles clean and orderly and serves as a lure for the man-of-war's prey. In return, the janitor fish receives shelter and food from the host, who somehow recognizes the little fish and leaves it unharmed in the general mayhem of the tentacles.

Why the Sidewinder Winds to the Side

Snakes walk on their ribs. Attached to the tip of each opposing pair of ribs is a horny shield that grips the ground. The snake pushes the set of ribs backwards, forcing the shield against the ground and levering itself forward. With up to 300 sets of ribs all working in tandem, the snake rows smoothly along like a racing shell in the Harvard Regatta. A snake needs rough ground to push the shields against. On a sheet of glass it would have no traction and would be immobilized. The horned rattlesnake of the American southwest, alias the sidewinder, lives in a slippery, sandy habitat that offers little resistance to allow it to propel itself forward. The sidewinder solves the friction problem by heaving itself sideways in a series of clumsy but effective leaps, leaving behind unmistakable and unique snakeprints.

Wandering Eyes
Flounder larvae, like the larvae of many other fishes, are transparent. After about four months they lose their transparency and begin to develop pigmentation. These tiny flounder swim in an upright orientation like the majority of other fishes and have eyes on opposite sides of their heads. However, as the young flounder develops its pigmentation an intricate rearrangement occurs. During a period of only three or four days, the eye on the right side of the head moves across the snout to the left side in an arc covering about 120 degrees. Simultaneously, the fish's entire body turns in such fashion that the pattern of upright swimming is no longer possible. Instead, the right side turns parallel with the ocean floor and the left side is exposed to view from above and develops intricate pigmentation for camouflage. The flat flounder is a bottom feeder and lives out its life with both eyes always looking up.

A Fish Out of Water
It was the ability of some fish to breathe air and the accompanying development of lungs during the Devonian period, beginning 400 million years ago, that led to the

evolution of the terrestrial (land) vertebrates. During the Devonian many bodies of fresh water became stagnant and dried up altogether. Under these conditions freshwater fish that could breath air, and perhaps move from a dried-up pond to a wet one, stood a good chance of survival.

The living lungfishes are relatives of those early air-breathing fishes. When in water the lungfish obtains oxygen like any other fish, by forcing water across its gills. When the lungfish surfaces for a breath of air, the gill covers close, the mouth opens, and air is forced into the lung as the mouth closes. The fish is able to avoid death by dehydration when the water in its lake or stream dries up by sealing itself up in a capsule and drastically reducing its metabolic rate. It may survive in such a state of suspended animation for as long as three years.

Certain fish, such as anabas, the climbing perch, are able to leave the ocean for a time. This Indian fish can climb trees, using its front fins as rudimentary arms to grasp the branches. It has been seen dragging its tail down roads and clumping through meadows on its stumpy fins like a miniature stilt-walker. The climbing perch is able to breathe on land because of a dispensation from nature: its gills can absorb oxygen from the air when the fish is out of the water.

The mudskipper goby is another land walker. It will climb out of the ocean, stick its little head up, and watch the world go by with its bulging, froglike eyes. It gobbles passing flies and other insects and hops off its perch, scooting into the forest or back into the water when frightened. The mudskipper breathes through the skin on its tail when on land, instead of using its gills. The adult mudskipper has a habit of alternately retracting one of its enormous bulging eyeballs into its head. It seems that the mudskipper does this because its gill slits begin to dry out and stick together after a certain amount of time on shore. Retracting one eye puts pressure on a reservoir of seawater in its inner ear and forces the water out to lubricate the gill slits.

Hold Your Breath

A number of birds and mammals spend a great deal of their lives on or under water. Most birds can stay submerged for only two or three minutes, and even the most accomplished diving bird, the emperor penguin, can remain underwater for only eighteen minutes. Whales are more efficient at exchanging the air in their lungs, and the bottlenose whale has been reported to dive for durations as long as two hours.

Helping Whales Breathe

Inhabiting the icy arctic regions of the north, the Narwal has a pair of tusks, only one of which develops to spiral and grow through the animal's mouth into a 7-to-8-foot-long spear. The narwal uses this tusk, or "unicorn," to cut holes in the ice so that it will have places to breath air under the ice-covered water.

Elephants Don't Sink

When an elephant walks along over soft sand or in mud it does not sink in as much as a man would despite its enormous weight. The distribution of weight per square foot of elephant feet is less than that of human beings. Also, because the shape and structure of their feet allow the foot to actually change shape when lifting out of tacky substances, no vacuum is created by the heavy step, and so the elephant can easily lift its feet out of mud.

Bird Body Design

If an animal has feathers, it's a bird. In addition, all birds have wings, although some bird species do not use their wings for flight. Flying birds, by design, carry as little extra body weight as possible. A flying bird's bones are incredibly lightweight and filled with air cavities. The skeleton of a frigate bird with a 7-foot wingspan weighs only 4 ounces, less than the weight of all its feathers.

One unique way of keeping body weight low is accomplished by allowing the sex organs to atrophy during the nonbreeding seasons. The sex organs of starlings weigh 1,500 times as much during mating season as they do during the rest of the year.

Feathered Friends

Like the nails and hair of humans, feathers are composed almost entirely of dead cells. A songbird usually has 1,500 to 3,000 feathers, but a swan may be covered by more than 25,000 of them. Feathers are masterpieces of design: they are very lightweight yet have a remarkable toughness and strength. They grow from buds similar to those that produce the scales on the bird's legs. In fact, bird feathers have evolved from the scales of their reptilian ancestors.

Nearly all birds go through a period of shedding and renewal of their feathers, a process called molting. Molting occurs annually, usually in the late summer after the nesting season. Many birds also undergo a second prenuptial molt in the spring, changing from dull to bright display plumage, which helps them attract a mate.

During molting most birds will lose and gradually replace their feathers over a period a several weeks. They lose flight and tail feathers in exact pairs, one from each side of the body, so that balance can be maintained. Most birds can continue to fly without difficulty during the molting period; however, ducks and geese find themselves completely grounded. The penguin is an exception to this orderly process: they molt all at once over the entire body.

How to Stay Warm

Most animals have an optimum body temperature, around which they function most efficiently. Below this temperature their metabolism slows down and the animal may become sluggish; above it an animal's metabolic rate increases rapidly, which may prove difficult for the animal to maintain for long periods of time since it literally burns up large amounts of its stored energy. For most species 117 degrees Fahrenheit is about the upper limit at which bodily processes remain viable. Fish in particular are very sensitive to temperature changes and have temperature sensors in the skin and brain. Catfish have been shown to respond to changes in temperature of less than 0.2 degrees Fahrenheit.

In warm-blooded animals the loss of body heat in cold weather can be reduced in a variety of ways. Large animals have an advantage over small ones, since it takes longer for interior body heat to reach the skin surface, where it is lost. The polar bear has layers of fat under its skin and spaces of air under its thick white fur, both of which provide much needed insulation to hold in their body heat. A polar bear's fur has a coating of oil to prevent wetness, and there is stiff fur on the bottom of its feet to help keep them warm and to allow the animal to walk on ice without slipping. Birds can conserve body heat by ruffing their feathers, which increases the trapped air insulation at the body's surface. Some mammals accomplish the same result by raising their hair.

Like other reptiles, lizards need to warm themselves after a cold night and often can be found basking in the morning sun in order to raise their body temperature. The warming effect of sunlight can be enhanced by an animal's coloration. A dark-colored body absorbs more heat than a light-colored one. A number of lizard species actually begin the day colored darkly and, as their temperature approaches the optimum, become paler in color. The desert iguana of the southwestern United States actually prefers a body temperature of 108 degrees Fahrenheit. The term *cold-blooded* certainly doesn't apply to these animals.

Animal Body Temperatures

A body temperature of 98.6 degrees Fahrenheit is considered normal for humans, with some natural variation in temperature throughout the day. The following two lists show just how much variation exists in normal body temperature among warm-blooded mammals and birds.

Mammal	Normal Body Temperature (°F)
Goat	103.8
Rabbit	101.3
Fur seal	99.9
Polar bear	99.1
African elephant	97.5
Blue whale	95.9
Three-toed sloth	91.7
Echidna (spiny anteater)	73.9

Bird	Normal Body Temperature (°F)
Western pewee	112.6
Canada jay	109.4
Wandering albatross	105.3
Owl	104.4
Hummingbird	104.2
Ostrich	102.6
King penguin	99.9
Arctic gull	93.2

Keeping Cool

In the often scorching-hot climates of India and Africa, elephants have learned to keep cool in many ways. They will submerge themselves in water, pack mud on their backs, and use their trunks to spray water over their entire body. By fanning their huge ears rapidly they are able to cool down the blood that courses through the large veins on the backside of their ears, thereby cooling down their entire body by as much as 9 degrees Fahrenheit. Rabbits, too, use their large ears to radiate body heat.

Desert Coolers

The camel's hump, contrary to popular belief, does not store water. The fatty tissue in the hump provides a reserve of food, but it also helps the camel to keep cool. Fat is a very good insulating material and generally is used to keep animals warm in cold climates. By concentrating almost all of the fat in the camel's body into a hump, the rest of the camel's body is able to radiate heat with high efficiency and this helps to keep the animal from overheating in the strong desert sun. Unusual for a mammal, the camel also has a variable body temperature which can change by as much as 10 degrees Fahrenheit during the course of the day.

Camels and many other desert animals are able to reduce the amount of direct heat from the sun that they are exposed to by continuously orienting themselves so that their narrow end points toward the sun.

Not a Sip
At least one mammal is able to survive without drinking water. The kangaroo rat eats nothing but seeds and other dry material, and this small desert inhabitant is able to produce all the water its body needs from the food it eats. All animals manufacture water in the process of metabolizing their food, since water is a by-product of the breakdown of carbohydrates. The kangaroo rat not only obtains all the water it needs through its metabolic process but is able to conserve the water it produces, because it has incredibly efficient kidneys that are capable of disposing of salts and other body wastes without excreting large amounts of water.

Beating the Heat
In the extreme heat of its desert home, the roadrunner will dispel excess body heat by fluttering a membrane between its lower jaws. The roadrunner also conserves water by excreting salts through glands near its eyes. A marvel of survival, descended from the cuckoo bird, a female roadrunner will toss any of its weaker nestlings into the air and swallow it whole in order to conserve scarce food for the stronger babies.

Solutions to a Salty Diet

Marine birds have evolved a unique way to excrete the large amount of salt in their food and in the seawater they drink. The problem is solved by special salt glands, one located above each eye. These glands are capable of excreting a highly concentrated solution of salt—up to twice the concentration of salt in seawater. The salt solution runs out the nostrils, giving gulls, petrels, and other sea birds a perpetual runny nose.

The Remarkable Tubeworm

The eyeless tubeworm could not see food if it was in the middle of it. Nor could it eat, since it doesn't have a mouth, nor digest food, since it doesn't have an alimentary canal. Nor could it expel waste, since it doesn't have an anus. It thrives on a diet of hydrogen sulfide, a poison so toxic it will kill a human. The deadly chemical is absorbed through the skin and is not used as food by the tubeworm, but by the bacteria that live within it. As the bacteria oxidize the hydrogen sulfide, the process releases energy that the bacteria thrive on. As they grow and multiply, the tubeworm digests the bacteria, always leaving enough of it to repeat the process.

Second Helpings

In some plant-eating mammals, such as rabbits, the gut has a spacious sidepocket called a cecum, which serves as a fermentation chamber and absorptive area. Hares, rabbits, and some rodents often eat their fecal pellets, giving the food a second pass through the fermenting action of the intestinal bacteria.

The Indestructible Rat

A rat can fall fifty feet and land on its feet uninjured.

It can jump two feet straight up and over four feet horizontally. It can crawl inside a pipe an inch and a half in diameter and squeeze through a hole the size of a quarter. When rats desert a sinking ship, they can swim continuously for days without tiring. A rat can enter a brick building by scaling the wall to the roof and penetrating it through a crack under a door or through a vent pipe. If that fails, it can chew its way inside. Rats have gnawed through wood, mortar, concrete, and brick and can chew their way through sheet metal over a half-inch thick.

Like all rodents, a rat's teeth grow continuously, and the rat actually gnaws for its life. With an average tooth-growth rate of four to five inches a year, if the rat doesn't gnaw them down every day, the teeth potentially will curve over and grow into the rat's brain, killing it. The gluttonous rat will eat anything in front of it: grain, fish, eggs, fowl, or meat.

The Ideal Seal Meal

Whereas humans divide eating into three or more periods of the day, many other animals spend most of their time finding and eating food wherever they can. Yet for seals and sea lions, feeding is something to get done with so they can go on to more important things like growing larger, mating, or maintaining territorial rights. Elephant seal pups nurse continually for about a month, then fast for three months, during which they live off body fat converted from the orgy of nursing. During this period the young seals are growing to full size, although they seem to be simply lying about the rocks and loafing. For these seals, eating in one concentrated period and storing the food as fat is an advantage, allowing them to make the best use of their time doing the things that will perpetuate the species.

Something For Every Body

Mammals that live in cold climates, and especially sea mammals whose bodies are insulated by a layer of blubber, have need for a lot of fat in their diets. There is a large difference in the composition of mother's milk among different mammals.

Animal	Milk fat content
Cow	4%
Dog	9%
Reindeer	17%
Blue Whale	40%
Grey Seal	53%

SENSORY
WONDERS

A Sensual Virtuoso

While many fishes have highly specialized skills that enable them to mate, find prey, and survive in the watery world they inhabit, the shark is by far the master of them all, a superfish with a range of abilities far beyond that of most undersea dwellers. This feared virtuoso of the deep combines many senses, all highly developed, in one entity. All the shark's talents are devoted to one goal: finding prey. The shark can sense electricity, and it hones in on the electric field generated by the body of the prey. It has an internal seismograph so sensitive it can detect the tiniest vibrations in the water caused by movements of his quarry. In addition, the shark's hearing is so acute it can hear fish swimming and the sound of the fish's muscles contracting. With eyesight much more powerful than a human's, the shark can see the various colors of the undersea world and interpret their meaning over great distances. Finally, the shark's sense of smell is so highly developed it can smell blood before it is within range of sight. To breathe, the shark has to keep moving continuously so that water flows through its respiratory system. This constant motion brings it into new environments continuously; it is a creature that never seems to rest in its predatory pursuits. This array of senses is responsible for the reputation of the shark as a mighty hunter.

Which Way Is Up?

Have you ever wondered how a clam, buried in six inches of sand, knows which way is up? The clam is able to orient itself in the earth's gravity by means of an ingenious organ called a statocyst. A tiny pebble floats in liquid inside a round bag that is lined with hairs connected to the clam's nervous system. When the clam is in a normal upright position, the pebble comes to rest on certain hairs inside the bag that transmit a signal to its nervous system that all is well. Should the clam be turned in any position other than the correct one, the pebble will roll around and stimulate other hairs that send an alarm telling the clam that it is out of its proper orientation.

The Jerboa's Tactile Radar

The desert jerboa leaps like a kangaroo, propelled swiftly along by two powerful hind legs. As it rockets across the desert it is vulnerable to surface irregularities and can have a serious fall if it miscalculates.

The jerboa solves the problem by trailing its extremely long whiskers along the ground, maintaining constant contact, like the electric boom that maintains contact with the overhead power lines on a trolley car. The whiskers act much like a cat's, transmitting a stream of tactile signals to the animal's brain.

The jerboa's tail also maintains constant contact with the ground, and when the whiskers signal danger it is used to steer the animal over or around the hazardous object.

SEEING

Variations in Eyelids

Snakes do not have eyelids; their eyes are covered by a clear scale, called the spectacle. The beaver is able to close its nose and ears when it dives beneath the water. Its eyes have transparent eyelids that serve as swimming goggles. Badgers have a second, transparent eyelid that they can see through when they are digging underground.

A Four-eyed Fish

Our eyes lack the ability to bulge out like those of a fish and to see clearly underwater. Fish have the same problem when they are above the water line. The anableps, a fish that swims on the surface of the water with half its eyeballs submerged and the other half above the water, developed an unusual solution to this dilemma. Each eye is in reality two eyes sharing the same eyeball and the same lens. Behind the lens, the part of the eye above water has a separate pupil and retina, as does the part of the eye below the water line. The four-eyed anableps watches the skies for predators and scopes out the water below for food simultaneously, keeping both worlds in focus.

Old Turret Eyes

The most mobile eyes in the animal kingdom belong to the chameleon. Mounted in conical turrets, the chameleon's eyes can detect potential prey in every possible direction without its having to move its head at all. The eyes are able to move independently of each other; while one eye scans the leaves and twigs above its head the other may be gazing straight in front, out to the side, or even downwards. When the chameleon sees an insect with one of its eyes, it instantly swivels its eye turrets so that both eyes are focused on the prey.

Powerful Eyesight

The huge eyes of the giant squid contain 1,000 million light detectors, one hundred times more than the human eye. Over half the squid's large brain is devoted to eyesight. Despite this concentration of resources, the squid does not see color—only a world of gray tones.

Simple Seeing

The tiny sea creature copilia, no bigger than the head of a pin, is the smallest animal capable of forming a visual image. The copilia's optic system is the link between the primitive eyespot and the more complex, image-forming eye. The copilia's miniscule body is transparent, and contains an interior lens onto which two exterior lenses focus light. Just like a television camera mounted on a wall, the interior lens of the copilia scans back and forth sending signals along a single optic fiber to its primitive brain. But don't try to find the copilia's interior lens unaided; it can be seen by humans only under magnification.

Large Eyes

The tarsier, a primitive tree-living primate of Southeast Asia, is roughly the size of a rat and is famous for its large eyes. In proportion to its body size, tarsiers have some of the largest eyes of any mammal. A human's eyes would have to be about 12 inches across to maintain the same proportion. In contrast, whales have the smallest eyes in proportion to their body size.

Seeing Colors

Color vision is widespread throughout the animal kingdom. Many fish, reptiles, and birds have true color vision. For a long time it was thought that cats, dogs, and cows were colorblind; however, experiments have shown that they too can see in color. Colors play a functional role in the lives of animals. For example, a frog, when threatened, will leap towards something blue (the color of water)—even something as simple as a blue cloth held by a human.

The retina of the human eye contains two types of light-sensitive cells, called rods and cones. The cones are able to distinguish different wavelengths of light and send this information to the brain, which processes the image into a color picture. There are three types of cones in the human eye; one is sensitive to blue light, one to green light, and the third to yellow-green and red light. Baboons and gorillas have cones that are sensitive to the same three portions of the color spectrum. Many other mammals, including squirrels and dogs, have only two types of cones in their retinas and cannot easily distinguish the difference between red and green. Individual squirrel monkeys have either two or three different types of cones, but these are selected from a possible choice of five types; each sensitive to a different hue.

Many animals have eyes that are sensitive to portions of the light spectrum that humans cannot detect without the use of machines. The stickleback fish has five different color-sensitive cones in its eyes, which enables it to discriminate more colors than humans can. The most highly developed color vision of any group of animals is found in birds. Not only do birds have five different color cones, but each cone has a drop of oil that further filters light into a very small band of wavelengths.

Seeing Red

The world of the piranha is that of black South American rivers filled with decaying vegetation; goldfish evolved in waters made red by the same source. Thus neither fish can see far using the normal range of the spectrum. Both the docile goldfish and the deadly piranha use the longer-wavelength infrared portion of the light spectrum, which penetrates the murky water of their natural habitat and allows them to see in semi-opaque environments.

This enhanced light sensitivity is an advantage to the piranha, who can see its prey but cannot be seen by the unlucky animal or fish until it is too late. Piranhas have been known to attack in schools of up to 1,000. In a frenzy of feeding they can strip an animal the size of a horse down to a skeleton in minutes, and even have been known to eat each other.

The goldfish, whose coloration acts as camouflage in the reddish waters, can spot predators approaching before they see it and find a place to hide until danger passes.

Hidden Signals

Insects such as bees can see ultraviolet light but have little sensitivity to the red part of the spectrum. As bees cruise over a meadow, the flowers in bloom stand out like beacons. Ultraviolet markings that are invisible to the eyes of vertebrates such as birds or humans guide the bees to the nectar in a symbiotic relationship that has fascinated scientists, poets, and others for centuries. Many jumping spiders have ultraviolet markings that can be seen only by members of their own species.

The tiny crab spider capitalizes on this difference between how certain species can see color. It sits in the middle of a flower and is able to change color so that it is an exact match of the flower and is invisible to its prey, the insects that come to suck the nectar. On the sides of the crab spider are two red spots, a clear warning to birds that the spiders are not edible. Because other insects are not sensitive to the red part of the spectrum, the spots are invisible to them and, unsuspecting and unaware of the danger, they land on the flower. The deadly disguise is perfect.

Polarized Light

When the sun's rays travel through the atmosphere of earth, some of the light becomes polarized so that the light waves vibrate only in one plane. Bees are able to detect the polarization plane of light and use this information as an aid in their navigation to and from the hive. Pigeons and some other birds also are capable of perceiving polarized light.

Visual Feats

Eagles, hawks, falcons, and other birds of prey have eyesight that is at least twice as acute as human vision. Golden eagles can spot a rabbit hopping on the ground from a distance of two miles. Peregrine falcons can see and hone in on a pigeon that is five miles away.

Special Vision

The swallowtail butterfly has light-sensitive cells on its sex organs, enabling it to "see" what is happening during the sex act. Since this species' coupling procedure is nearly as complex as docking a spaceship, the sight cells play an important role in making sure that all goes well.

Light Detectors

The entire bodies of many primitive invertebrate animals such as jelly-fish, coral, sea anemones, worms, starfish, and sea urchins are sensitive to light. Even if their primitive eyes—merely a dense collection of photosensitive cells—are completely covered, the outer surfaces of these creatures remain sensitive to light.

The Spider with Eight Eyes

The spider with the best eyesight is the eight-eyed jumping spider. Since the jumping spider is a hunter and does not weave a web, it must rely on its vision to see and catch its prey. Two pairs of eyes on both sides of its head give the jumping spider excellent peripheral vision; a smaller pair of eyes in the front are distance estimators, and the larger main eyes form the image.

These eight-eyed hunting spiders can see clearly up to one foot away and can jump twenty times their own length to catch food.

Jumping spiders communicate with each other using visual signs such as waving their legs in particular ways indicating the desire to mate or warning of danger. They will also pirouette from side to side during a courtship dance.

HEARING

Hearing Sensitivity

It is said that small animals squeak and large ones rumble because the smaller the animal's head, the higher the frequency of sounds it can receive and transmit. The reason for this is that in order to determine which direction a sound is coming from, the brain must distinguish which ear hears it first and the time difference between its reception by both ears. So the closer the animal's ears are together, the shorter the wavelength and therefore the higher the frequency necessary for good discrimination.

There is a vast difference in the range of frequencies

that various animals can hear. The frequency of sound is measured in cycles per seconds, or hertz.

Animal	Hearing Range (cycles per second)
Bat	1,000–210,000
Dolphin	150–200,000
Cat	60–65,000
Dog	15–50,000
Human	20–20,000
Elephant	5–18,000
Frog	50–10,000
Pigeon	0.1–15,000

Navigating by Sound

In the late 1930s scientists discovered the secret of how some bats can see in the dark. The bouncing echoes of the bat's ultrasonic squeaks allows it to navigate in a cave filled with thousands of other bats without ever crashing into anything.

Once this secret entered the realm of known fact, scientists began wondering how the bat avoided going batty from listening to the sound of its own squeaks and exactly how it managed to hear the faint echoes so clearly.

The bat has an astonishing switch, in the form of a tiny muscle, inside its ear. As the bat begins his shriek, the muscle contracts, pulling the ear bone away from the eardrum, the oval window that goes into the inner ear. In effect, this muscle unplugs the bat's hearing system and makes it deaf for a fraction of a second.

The on-off-on switch works continuously, as long as the bat is shrieking, and is timed to match the frequency of the shrieks, which increases as the bat nears its prey. The bat hears the *echo* of its cries, not the actual shriek.

Locating Sound

Animals have two ears in order to locate the direction from which a sound has come. A sound to the right will reach the right ear slightly before it reaches the left, and the brain is able to interpret this miniscule difference in timing to calculate the location of the sound. One species has taken ear placement a step further. The barn owl can tell not only whether a sound has come from the right or left, but also whether the source of the sound is above or below. It is able to do this because one of its ears is placed slightly lower on its head than the other.

Ear Movement

A dog has seventeen muscles in each ear, which can be used to raise and lower the ear or swivel it in different directions. The human ear, by comparison, has only nine muscles in it, none of which actually work very well except for those people who can wiggle their ears.

Internal Ears

Although snakes do not have external ears, they are not totally deaf. They do have internal ears, and recent studies have shown that at least in a limited range of low frequencies (100 to 700 hertz), hearing in snakes compares well with that of most lizards. A snake doesn't have much need for ears because it has other sensory apparatus that work better for it. Being a ground-bound creature, the snake is worried about something stepping on him or eating him, as well as about his next meal. Snakes have a system to detect vibrations on the ground that serves their needs better than ears.

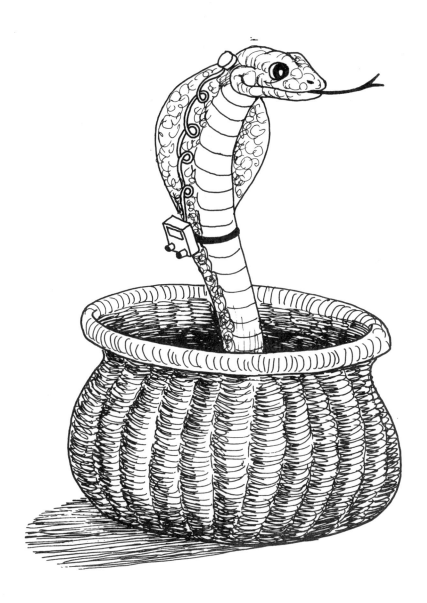

TASTE
AND
SMELL

Good Taste

Taste is the difference between gluttony and art—it's what separates those who eat to live from those who live to eat. Among animals, taste is stripped of its aesthetic value and, like so many other features, serves as an important tool for survival.

A toad will stuff a juicy earthworm into its mouth and contentedly watch for another. If a baby grass snake, the approximate size of an earthworm, crawls into the toad's field of vision, the toad will grab it and put it into its mouth. A few seconds later the toad will frantically spit out the snake, because it secretes a fluid that causes the toad's taste buds to sound an alarm. When the snake becomes an adult, it will dine on toads.

Parrots will taste all food with their tongue before swallowing it. The parrot only has about 400 taste buds, yet the taste test can tell it whether a piece of fruit is unripe, overripe, or just right.

Some insects, such as the red Burnet moth, contain prussic acid, which to a bird must taste like a spicy hot pepper. In one experiment, using birds raised in captivity that had never before seen a Burnet moth, a bird picked up the moth as if to eat it, then suddenly dropped it like a hot potato. The bird spent sometime hopping about, eating wet grass, and wiping its beak on the cage.

Taste Buds

The average human being has about 9,000 taste buds. Compare this to those found in the animal world:

Animal	Tastebuds
Catfish	100,000
Cow	35,000
Rabbit	17,000
Pig	15,000
Goat	15,000
Bat	800
Bird	200

The Taste Buds of Fish

Of all the various senses possessed by animals, the chemical senses of taste and smell are probably the most important for survival. In all likelihood, the first senses to evolve in early animals were those that were receptive to chemical stimulation. All animals need to eat, and ultimately it is a substance's chemical composition that determines whether or not it is food.

In addition to having taste buds in the mouth, many fish actually have taste buds on the surface of their bodies. The sea-robin even has specially modified pectoral fins, the tips of which are studded with taste receptors. As it moves around on the ocean floor the sea-robin samples the bottom surface with its fin rays, and when it touches something tasty it goes after it by digging with its mouth.

Buried Rabbits

When a mother rabbit has to leave her babies, she digs a hole in the earth and partially buries her children in the loose soil. Because baby rabbits have almost no scent, a passing fox will not be able to smell them despite its keen sense of smell. The fox's sense of smell is so acute that it can locate caches of dead birds and their eggs it had buried solely by smell, since its memory is not as highly developed as its nose.

Dog Noses

Domestic dogs have inherited their incredibly acute sense of smell from their wolf ancestors. Wolves are able to detect the scent of a deer from a distance of over one mile. In the wild, this sense of smell can mean the difference between life and death.

A dog's sense of smell is vastly more sensitive than a human's. When a man walks barefoot over the ground he leaves in each footprint four-billionths of a gram of odorous sweat. Even so, this is more than enough for any dog to track accurately. An average human has five million olfactory sensory cells that are receptive to smell, but this is a small number compared to that of dogs. Even different dog breeds have different numbers of olfactory sensory cells; for example, a dachshund has about 125 million, a fox terrier has 147 million, and a sheepdog has 220 million.

In one experiment with bloodhounds, researchers tried to confuse the dog by allowing relatives of the person tracked to criss-cross the path. The bloodhound ignored all dummy trails and kept tracking his quarry. After centuries of breeding and training, the bloodhound possesses a sense of smell a million times more powerful than that of humans. The membrane inside its nose that senses odors is over 30 times larger than the similar membrane in a human nose. When the bloodhound sniffs a trail, his long ears, fleshy dewlap (chin), and the shape of his head combines to create a cuplike area that isolates the odor from surrounding smells. The bloodhound is so sensitive that he is sometimes unable to follow a fresh trail because the odors are too strong and must wait until the trail "cools" before setting off in pursuit. The bloodhound's sense of smell is so acute and consistently accurate that it is the only animal whose "testimony" can be used as evidence in United States courts.

Bloodhound Bird

What the kiwi lacks in sight it makes up for with astonishing senses of smell and touch. When it comes out at night to feed on worms the kiwi will walk along, continually tapping the ground with the tip of its bill. As soon as it has detected a worm, it plunges its nostril-tipped bill into the ground and drags the worm out.

The extreme efficiency of the kiwi's sense of smell has been demonstrated by putting an earthworm on the ground in front of it and letting the worm crawl away for several yards while holding the bird still. On being released, the kiwi taps and sniffs the ground following the path of the worm with the accuracy of a bloodhound.

How a Snake Smells with Its Tongue

For years it was thought that the snake's forked tongue was used to feel along in the dark, like the whiskers of a cat. Another popular belief was that it was poisonous. The forked tongue, which the snake can flick in and out without opening its mouth, through a gap in its lips, is actually an organ of smell.

The tongue flicks out and waves around to attract a few odor molecules floating in the air. The two forks of the tongue are inserted briefly into two cavities in the top of the snake's mouth called Jacobson's organ. Sensors inside this organ immediately analyze the molecules and send the appropriate message to the snake's brain. The tongue can detect smells that signal danger, approaching prey, or the presence of a mate long before the snake can see or hear the source of the odors.

EXTRAORDINARY PHYSIOLOGY

Finding the Blood

The dreaded vampire bat uses echolocation to find its prey. But how does it know what part of the body to affix itself to so it doesn't latch onto a horse's hoof or a cow's horn, instead of a juicier part of the anatomy? It does this with a leaf, which is affixed to its nose. The nose-leaf is heat sensitive and is separated from the bat's body heat by a layer of insulating tissue that causes it to be colder than the rest of the body. Once the prey is located, the heat sensor in the bat's nose guides it straight to the part of the body where the warm blood is closest to the surface.

The vampire bat's teeth have sharp cutting edges, and after the vampire locates its sleeping victim it makes a short incision in the victim's skin with its upper teeth. As soon as the blood starts to flow, it curls up the edges of its tongue and laps up the blood. The vampire bat's saliva contains an anticoagulant, and with its voracious appetite, it will continue to drink the blood of its victims until its stomach is swollen and it is almost too heavy to fly away.

X-Ray Vision

Dolphins use a form of echolocation similar to that of the bat. As they swim along, they emit short pulses of sound at ranges up to 200,000 hertz at the rate of 10 to 200 per second, depending on what they are doing. The sound travels through the water and through the tissues of fish in its way, bouncing back only when it hits bone. Echolocation gives the dolphin the equivalent of an X-ray view of the ocean, enabling it to identify prey by the living skeleton and decide whether it wants to eat the fish or ignore it.

Sounding the Water

Noctilio, a Panamanian bat, has taken a step further the famous echolocation used by its cousins to catch insects on the wing. Aiming at the water, Noctilio has developed a form of sonar. By aiming its echolocation at the pools and streams in the jungle, it can "see" fish swimming in the water below it. Swooping down in the dark, it catches the unsuspecting prey for dinner. Other bats in the Panamanian jungles prefer frog's legs and specialize in following the mating calls of singing frogs. If a lovesick frog gets carried away with its mating song and lingers too long, it will soon get carried off by a bat flying around in the night air and listening hungrily to the croaking chorus below it.

Many species of bats dine exclusively on insects, and a single bat can consume as many as 3,000 insects in one night. The cumulative members of one bat colony in Texas have been proven to eat 250,000 pounds of insects nightly.

Safety in Numbers

Watching a school of fish is like watching a precision drill team. Each fish turns on an unseen command, maintaining the same distance from others. The school disperses and reforms as if it had rehearsed. Blindfolded fish show no loss of this ability, proving that sight is not what causes the precise movements. Some schools of herring are a dozen miles long and contain millions of fish, all equidistant from each other and moving in precision formation.

All fish have a lateral line system in their bodies that allow them to hear infrasound, low-level vibrations in the water made by the movement of other fish. These sensors are made up of a system of channels under the skin and along the side of the body and head that are studded with groups of hair cells, with the ends of the hairs embedded in a thick fluid. These receptors are highly sensitive to movements of the surrounding water. By balancing the infrasound signals, the fish keep their place in the formation and the entire school moves as one to avoid an obstacle or impending danger.

Fish Antennae

Many fish are able to detect prey using their lateral system as a sort of antenna. Shrimp vibrate at 40 hertz, the frequency their archenemy Pagothenia, an Antarctic fish, is tuned to. Pagothenia hones into the shrimp's wavelength and goes directly to its next meal. The shark is very sensitive to frequencies around 200 hertz, which is, coincidentally, the same as the vibrations of a helicoptor rotor. Rescues at sea are made more dangerous by the song of the rotor blades summoning sharks in the area to the scene.

One variety of deep sea angler fish has a fishing line growing out of its nose that is four times the length of the fish's body. Unlike other angler fish, this one doesn't use the line to attract prey but rather as a deep-sea antenna, searching the depths for telltale vibrations in the water. As soon as the fish detects some activity with this antenna, it heads straight for the source of the vibration, trailing the fishing line behind.

Electric Detectives

Many lower animal organisms, such as bacteria, are known to orient themselves in artificial electric fields. A number of fish species also have an innate electrical sensitivity, which they use in locating prey. The dogfish is particularly electrosensitive and is capable of detecting its prey fish, even when they are buried in the sand, by the local distortion they cause in the earth's natural electrical field. The sense organs that are used for this are called the *ampullae Lorenzini*, named after the anatomist who discovered them. These organs, which occur widely distributed over the body surface, but especially on the head of sharks, are thought to be evolutionary derivatives from lateral line organs.

Magnetic Fish

Just over five feet in length, with poor vision, the African knife fish is a peculiar creature that senses its environment by emanating an electric field. Think of the knife fish as a 5-foot-long magnet. The fish's head is the positive pole and the tail is the negative. Pulsing at from 3 to 10 volts at the rate of 300 impulses each second, the knife fish swims in a self-created force-field too weak to have any effect on other animals but strong enough so that disturbances in the field can be sensed by the knife fish. By holding a simple magnet above the surface of the water it is possible to attract a knife fish, who will approach the magnet and wait for something to happen.

When a knife fish encounters a strange object, the lines of the electric field are either bent apart to go around a poor electric conductor or drawn together if the object is a good conductor of electricity. Through a method not yet understood, the knife fish interprets these minute fluctuations in the feeble current and "sees" the object well enough to determine whether it is approaching food, an approaching enemy or mate, or a barrier. If one knife fish encounters another, both will stop transmitting signals for a few seconds and then resume on different noncompeting frequencies.

The knife fish has another unique ability: it does not use its tail to propel itself as other fish do, but moves along by undulating a long fin that runs the length of the top of the body. By reversing the direction of the undulations, the knife fish is able to swim backwards.

Magnetic Senses

A number of animals, including many migratory birds, homing pigeons, snails, and honeybees, have been shown to be sensitive to magnetic fields. Studies done with caged robins have shown that, in the absence of visual clues such as sunlight, they are able to correctly orient their escape attempts for migration, guided only by earth's magnetic field. One peculiar finding of these experiments is that robins do not seem to be able to distinguish the north and south poles of a magnetic field. There have been indications, however, that the birds can sense the downward inclination of the earth's magnetic field, which is northward in northern latitudes and southward in southern ones. Experiments done in the 1970s, in which magnets were attached to homing pigeons' heads, demonstrated that when the sky was clouded over and the sun was not visible, the pigeons were confused and disoriented when flying back to their home loft.

Heat Detectors

Rattlesnakes, moccasins, and other pit vipers can "see" in the dark. In the total absence of light they locate their next meal by body heat, given off in the invisible (to humans) infrared portion of the spectrum. Two tiny pinholes located between the nostrils and the eyes focus on infrared radiation. When heat is detected, the radiation "image" is projected on a small screen inside the snake's head. The back of the screen is a grid of 7,000 nerve endings sensitive to heat changes as slight as .003 degree Fahrenheit, and the system reacts to any temperature changes within thirty-five milliseconds.

Information recorded on the screen is sent to the snake's vision system in its brain, enabling the snake to see the outline of the heat-emitting animal as a glowing, red silhouette. Locating a well-camouflaged animal is easy for the snake, though he may not see it visually. Snakes equipped with this system can locate living things in total darkness. The speed with which the system works is so great that after the snake begins his strike, it immediately senses any movement of the animal. Course corrections are made en route, so the target cannot escape. There are additional heat sensors inside the snake's mouth that aid the guidance system even after it has opened its mouth to strike and the infrared sensors on its face have inadvertently pointed it in the wrong direction.

An Electric Bill

Add another oddity to the collection of oddities that make up the duck-billed platypus: it is the only mammal who can detect electricity. It does this with sensors embedded in its bill.

The platypus loves shrimp, and the freshwater shrimp it feeds on generate an electrical current of one-thousandth of a volt each time they flip their tails, more than enough to register on the platypus' electric-bill-meter, which detects fields as low as 500-millionths of a volt.

Pressure Sensors

Pigeons are extremely sensitive to barometric pressure and can detect the differences in air pressure that correspond to as little as a 100-foot change in elevation. The barometer, located in the middle ear, also exists in other birds and some sharks. Penguins have a particularly large pressure-sensitive organ, and perhaps they use this sense to gauge the depth of the water in which they dive.

Getting Along in the Animal Kingdom

ANIMALS COOPERATING

No animal is an island unto itself; animal societies are astonishingly well-developed when we consider the general lack of conflict among different species even amidst the most adverse conditions for survival. The only enemies animals have are hunger, cold, and the predatory survival instincts of other species. Often, in fact, one species will help another, and some animals will even endanger their own lives for the sake of rescuing another.

There are probably more ideal partnerships among animals than among humans. A careful study of dolphin cooperation and communication, or of elephant herds and their familial behaviors toward one another, should put to rest any notion that animals do not relate meaningfully to one another or that animal groups are merely numbers of isolated individual creatures roaming together without any sense of community.

Many animals have even learned to cooperate with those of another species, with both partners deriving some significant benefit from the association. In return for help in finding food or for keeping the other clean, animals offer each other protection and assistance in the struggle for existence. They have evolved to find ways to live and breathe and move together in some ways that should be the envy of humans.

How the Hippopotamus Feeds the Egret
The buff-backed heron, more commonly known as the cattle egret, is a beautiful white bird with long plumes sweeping back from the top of the head. These lovely egrets are nearly always found in the company of cattle, antelopes, buffalo, and hippopotamuses. As the grazing animals eat their way slowly through the grass, the egrets get very excited and are constantly busy running around the huge beasts' legs and diving into the grass, not in the least concerned about getting trampled. Careful study of the scene will reveal the purpose of the egrets' strange behavior· their favorite food is the grasshopper, so well camouflaged in the grass that it is impossible for the birds to see them until the grasshoppers fly away from the munching quadrupeds.

The Ox-pecker and the Rhinoceros
The ox-pecker, much smaller than the egret that hangs out with the hippo, is the size of a starling. These little birds ride piggyback (or hippo-back or ox-back) and derive their entire diet from the insects disturbed by their hosts, from ticks that grow in the hosts' skin, and from the numerous flies that settle on their partner's body. The only time ox-peckers will leave their comfortable living perch is when someone disturbs them or when their host is attacked by a bigger beast. At other times they never descend to the ground or fly to the trees; they spend almost their entire lives on the backs of antelopes, cattle, buffalo, zebra, and rhinoceroses. The ox-pecker males and females even

conduct their courtship and mating rituals on the backs of their accommodating friends

Astonishing transformations in the physiology of these birds have evolved over the eons and millenia to assist them in staying astride their beast-host—even when the quadruped wades into deep water, for example. Like the exceptionally sharp claws of the woodpecker, the ox-pecker's claws and strong-gripping toes enable it to run all over the large animal's back without losing balance. Its tail is extremely stiff, giving the little bird additional support as it clings to the flanks of its host.

The large grazing animals happily tolerate the hungry little birds because of the benefit they derive from having ticks and parasites removed and also because the ox-pecker chirps a clear warning to its host if a man approaches from even several hundred yards away. Humans are the only animals, however, that the little bird will warn of, and for this reason the ox-pecker is much hated by big-game hunters.

The Butterfly and the Ant

Before entering the chrysalis stage, the caterpillar that will become the blue butterfly seems to vanish completely from its breeding place. Not long thereafter the beautiful blue butterfly suddenly will appear. For hundreds of years no one knew exactly from where the butterfly emerged. All attempts to breed these butterflies in captivity failed. At first the caterpillars would thrive on their preferred diet of wild thyme flowers, but suddenly, just before the chrysalis stage, they would cease to eat anything offered to them, wander around their enclosures, lie down, and soon die.

This mystery was not resolved until 1915 when one great authority on butterflies was searching for caterpillars among wild thyme plants and pulled up a plant that was growing on an ant's nest. There, lying in a chamber of the now-exposed nest, was the long-sought chrysalis.

Careful observation of the blue caterpillar's behavior revealed the secret of its disappearance. Just before the chrysalis stage, when the caterpillar leaves the thyme plant, it wanders aimlessly about until it meets an ant or two. The ants show great interest, because the caterpillar has temporarily developed a gland on its back that secretes a sweet fluid when touched by an ant's antenna.

After teasing the ants with some of this sweet food, the caterpillar will hunch itself up in such a way that an ant can easily pick it up and carry it back to the nest. Inside the nest the caterpillar, with its tasty secretions, is an honored guest, and the ants feed it their own grubs. After growing to full size in several weeks in the safe and comfortable chamber of the ant nest, the caterpillar stops eating and develops a chrysalis in order to begin its metamorphosis into a butterfly. In springtime the adult butterfly emerges from the chrysalis case, climbs out of the ant nest and up the nearest grass stalk, and flies away.

Open Wide, Please

Leeches affix themselves to the gums of crocodiles, causing major oral maladies for the toothsome reptile. To floss his teeth and rid himself of the pests, the crocodile lumbers onto a riverbank, lies down, opens his enormous mouth, and waits. A spur-winged plover soon flies straight into the gaping maw and nonchalantly strolls around on the crocodile's tongue, inspecting the gums for juicy leeches.

The crocodile regularly eats birds of all species, but it somehow recognizes the plover as a friend and puts up with the inconvenience of having the little bird inside its mouth. As the feathered dental hygienist flies away, the crocodile slithers back into the muddy stream, smiling gratefully. As part of its package of services the plover keeps a sharp eye out for enemies of the crocodile. When danger threatens it sounds the alarm, sending crocodiles splashing for cover and ensuring a continuation of the leech supply for the plover.

Deep-sea Hitchhikers

The remora, or shark-sucker, has an odd but effective way of protecting itself from predators and finding new areas to feed in. The remora has an oval suction cup on its head, with which it affixes itself to a larger fish. The fish the little remora chooses to supply it with free rides and protection from predators is the bully of the deep, the murderous shark. The remora's colors change to match perfectly the skin of the shark, making the hitchhiker invisible to any other fish foolish enough to investigate.

Contrary to popular belief, the remora does not suck the blood of the shark. It does provide a useful service by eating the parasites that infest the skin of many sharks, accounting for the benign attitude the shark has to what otherwise would be a tasty morsel. While the shark is busy eating its prey, the remora may detach to feed on the leftovers and then hop on the shark again for another ride. While the little remora prefers sharks, it isn't fussy about what vehicle it bums a ride on, often affixing itself to the sides of freighters and luxury cruise ships.

The Bush Buck's Guardians

Baboons are the sentinels for the bush buck antelope in Africa. When leopards approach the watering holes where the bush buck drinks, the baboons will leap from tree to tree screaming a loud alarm. The baboons not only warn the bush bucks of impending danger, but also drop treetop leaves and fruits for the ground-locked bush buck to eat.

A Joint Search for Honey

The African honeyguide bird loves to eat honeybee grubs. The problem is its small size, which prevents it from breaking into the well-fortified bee nests. When the honeyguide finds a hive it flits about until it locates a honey badger, or ratel, who dotes on honey. It excitedly tells the honey badger all about its find and leads the animal to the site. The thick skin of the honey badger is impervious to bee stings. It calmly tears the nest apart with its long claws while the little honeyguide hovers overhead, waiting to grab some grub. Humans in the area who recognize the honeyguide's message run to get the honey before the honey badger does. Regardless of who gets the honey, the honeyguide accomplishes its mission.

A Dog in Sheep's Clothing

At first glance the big and shaggy Anatolian sheep dogs look like the sheep they guard. Raised with the flock from puppyhood, they are treated as sheep by their shepherd masters. They romp with the flock, eat with them, and sometimes try to copulate with them. The dogs grow up thinking they are sheep.

The idea behind this treatment is to make the dogs loyal to the sheep. When a strange person or dog approaches, the Anatolians suddenly separate themselves from their docile flock and revert to their aggressive birthright as dogs by driving off the outsiders.

Cleaning and Feeding

As the seaweed curtains part on our undersea theater, a large, dark-colored, melon-shaped fish partially hidden behind some coral branches emerges. It is watching the antics of a tiny, garishly colored wrasse as the smaller fish bobs and weaves like a punch-drunk fighter. Wide-eyed, its mouth opening and closing, the larger fish slowly emerges into open water. As it comes into full view of the excited smaller fish, it begins to turn from a dark color to a pale blue. The color change now reveals dozens of tiny parasites affixed to its body, which stand out clearly against the blue backdrop. The hungry wrasse fearlessly munches on this delicious smorgasbord until the larger fish is completely clean and parasite free.

During the cleaning/feeding process, the large fish seems in the thrall of a trance. It floats about in the water, sometimes lying on its side and occasionally standing on its head as the busy wrasse works it over. Small fishes like the wrasse are usually lunch for the large fish, but the latter turns away to find a meal of its own, leaving the wrasse untouched. The wrasse knows it is safe and meticulously cleans the entire body of the host, even around its large, toothy mouth. As the newly cleaned fish glides gratefully away, the wrasse, who keep its fellow fish clean and neat, is already seeking its next customer.

Our Next Best Friend

The dog's role as our best friend has been secure for millennia. A dog is the only creature who fairly leaps out of its skin with joy just because a person walked into the house. But coming up in the next century may be an animal contender with a different agenda. Elaborating on methods used to condition consumers to buy certain advertised products, and developed further into training techniques for circus animals, modern techniques of animal conditioning have been enhanced with lasers and other devices to train monkeys to act as assistants to people with physical disabilities or handicaps.

Monkeys are now being used experimentally to turn lights on and off, dust the furniture, use a carpet sweeper, put records on the stereo, turn on the television and select the right channel, and open the refrigerator, take out food and drinks, and feed them to their human charges. When the meal is over the monkey takes out a book, puts it on a reading shelf in front of the human, and turns the pages on command, combing the reader's hair as he reads.

Next they may be teaching the monkey to walk the dog.

Down on the Aphid Farm

In return for being allowed to remain in the safety and shelter of ants' nests, greenfly aphids allow the ants to milk them. To milk the aphid, the ant stands behind it and strokes its body many times in quick succession with its antennae. A drop of clear, tasty fluid appears from the hind end of the aphid's body, which is soon lapped up by the grateful ants.

Small black lawn ants actually farm these aphids, looking after their herds of aphids as a dairy farmer tends his cows. The ants build little mud sheds on stems and on leaf stalks so that the aphids may hide from their enemies. At night the ants carry some of their herd back to the ant nest, returning them gently to the plants in the morning. Ants increase the size of their herd by fetching more aphids from plants further away and bringing them back to their aphid farm.

During the autumn ants collect the tiny dark aphid eggs and carry them to their nest for protection during the winter. When spring comes, the aphid eggs are taken out of the ant nest and placed carefully on the correct food plants, where the ants will farm a new colony of aphids to milk throughout the summer.

Communications among animals takes many different forms: birds, whales, and crickets have elaborate songs; fireflies and some fishes flash; dogs wag their tails; lions roar; and snakes and cats hiss. Animals' communication takes advantage of all the senses: sight, sound, touch, and the chemical sense of smell and taste.

VOICE
AND
SONG

Dolphin Conferences

It has often been observed throughout the seas that before dolphins initiate any group action they have a conference. A group of dolphins, called a pod, will float together just below the surface of the water, facing each other. They politely take turns vocalizing until a consensus is finally reached.

The Joy of Learning

Some dolphins are highly intelligent, and it is well known to dolphin observers and trainers that these remarkable animals respond to training because it is fun rather than just to please humans or to obtain food. Dolphins are capable of imitation, memorization, and learning by observation. They have on many occasions demonstrated their ability to communicate their experiences, solve complicated problems, and perform complex tasks. Numerous professional dolphin trainers have claimed that there is a point in the training at which dolphins take over and begin to audition new tricks and ideas that the trainer may not have been eliciting. Dolphin trainers often remark, "The dolphin trained me!"

Undersea Noise Pollution

In researching the behavior of whales for submarine warfare, the Navy discovered that pods of whales communicate across thousands of miles of ocean to other pods to warn them, for example, of the approach of a whaling ship. More recently it has been observed that whales are no longer communicating effectively over great distances, perhaps due to the incessant underwater roar of thousands of huge ships throughout the world's oceans.

Whale Songs

Whales communicate with each other using various sounds that are complex and audible to other whales over great distances. The whale vocalizations vary depending on whether the speaker is addressing a male or a female, is in danger of some sort, or is just communicating about food or weather conditions. A careful study of whale language recordings shows a mass of punctuated, prefixed sounds that indicate very complicated communication.

The male humpback whale sings a mating song so poignant that a best-selling commercial recording of it is available. In mating season, the whales gather together for a songfest that can go on for a full day. A typical song lasts ten to twenty minutes and has up to eight recognizable themes, repeated over and over. Whales sing songs that evolve and change over their lifetime. Each group of whales has its own songs, and the themes of last year's songs are heard in subsequent years, indicating a memory of favorite melodies. As the season progresses the whales work on the songs, adding phrases and deleting phrases and polishing the melodies.

Fin whales emit a sound so low and so loud it can be heard hundreds of miles away. Scientists believe that if fin whales use a peculiar property of the ocean, their calls may be heard by other whales thousands of miles away. At certain depths, sound does not disperse normally but is concentrated and channeled because of a certain combination of water pressure, temperature, and salinity. If a whale can "shout" into one end of this undersea channel, it is possible for the sound to travel across the ocean before it becomes too weak to be heard by other whales. Whether or not the whales take advantage of this phenomenon is not known, and the full extent of whale communication is only dimly understood, but, clearly, it is far more complex than was once thought.

Insect Sounds

The world of insects is a deafening cacophony of buzzes, chirps, clicks, and hums, so it is not surprising to learn that sound is an important means of insect communication. Two of the noisiest insects, the cicada and the cricket, have no ears on their heads. Instead the cicada listens through ears on its belly and the cricket hears through its knees.

As she listens through her knees to the cheery chirping of the male's mating call, the female cricket makes her way toward the sound until the lovers are united. To reinforce his chances of being heard above the cacophony of the forest, the mole cricket builds a horn-shaped amplifier out of earth in a little burrow he makes for this purpose. Inside the burrow he hollows out a chamber, testing it with his mating call until the sound in the camber resonates at 3,000 hertz, the frequency to which the female's knees are tuned.

While the enthusiastic cricket advertises his love plans by rubbing his specially equipped wings together, the male fruit fly does the same thing by simply beating his wings. Although there are over 2,000 species of fruit fly and they all look pretty much alike, they never interbreed, because each subspecies operates on a different frequency. When a lovesick male fruit fly spies a female, he begins to beat his wings to the rhythm of his courting song. When she responds by beating her own wings, the male listens to find out if she is on the same frequency. If not, he continues searching for a female of his subspecies.

Spiders gauge the size of enemies or prospective mates by the sounds they emit. They sometimes will appear when a certain tune is played on the piano, confusing the vibrations of the piano wires with those of female spiders.

Can Monkeys Talk?

Attempts to communicate between humans and primates by sign language have been underway for some time, with intriguing results, but can monkeys talk to each other in the wild in a language we don't understand? After scientific investigation, the random chatter of the jungle gives way to the conclusion that, at least among certain species of monkeys, there is verbal communication.

The vervet monkeys of Amboseli National Park, north of Mount Kilimanjaro in Kenya, have different alarm calls for leopards, eagles, and snakes, all natural enemies of the monkeys. After recording these cries naturalists played them back to the monkeys. When the leopard alarm was played the monkeys raced to the outermost branches of the trees, where a leopard could not gain a foothold. When the eagle alarm was played they ran to hide where they would not be visible from the air. When the snake alarm was played the monkeys peered anxiously into the underbrush, watching for the approaching reptile. Unveiling a stuffed leopard before the surprised flock set them off on a chorus of leopard alarms lasting an hour. Research into this fascinating subject continues, but it is clear that monkeys, like many other animals, have a rudimentary language that may be far more complicated than we yet understand.

Bee Language
A honeybee that bumbles into a field of flowers loaded with nectar and pollen returns to the hive and tells fellow worker bees not only what he has found, but where it is and how far away. The bee does this with a rudimentary bee language in the form of a dance. The other workers gather around the town crier, who informs her colleagues of what she found and where they can find it by the motions she makes during the dance sequence. The workers immediately head straight for the bonanza field.

The Elephant Telephone
Aspects of elephant behavior have long puzzled scientists. A herd, scattered over huge distances, will suddenly come together to help an elephant in distress, or an entire herd will simultaneously begin to move away from impending danger, with no apparent communication between its members. Elephants communicate over long distances by means of infrasound, using sound frequencies below the hearing range of humans and most other animals. A low rumble beginning in the elephant's throat, amplified by a hollow space beneath the forehead, is directed outward where it is heard clearly by other elephants, sometimes miles away.

Noisy Fish
In 1942, during World War II, buoys wired with the latest in underwater sound detectors were placed in Ches-

apeake Bay in order to listen for German U-boats intent on destroying Washington, D.C. On a balmy May evening, the sound detectors went off their scales with what was interpreted to be the sounds of the entire German submarine fleet. The Navy and Coast Guard swung into action and dropped enough depth charges into the bay to destroy several underwater armadas. No submarine debris surfaced, but the next day the bay was covered with the bodies of millions of dead fish.

Meanwhile, the harbors on the Pacific coast were fitted out with a new secret weapon: acoustic mines set to explode at the sound of an approaching ship propeller. In one night every mine exploded at once, yet there was never a ship in sight.

These fiascos were caused by the human conceit that, since we normally cannot hear anything underwater, fish can't talk. Both coastal alarms, however, were set off by the cacophony of schools of millions of fish.

Since then we have discovered that the oceans are filled with an unimaginable din of fishes calling, croaking, singing, thumping, and clicking millions of messages. Only now are these messages being recognized as a form of communication, and serious research into just what these sounds might mean is taking place.

In their efforts to understand the varieties of underwater communication by fish, scientists have deciphered the soft chirping recorded from schools of herring. The length and timing of the herring chirps signal different things. Herring can signal each other to fall into schooling formation, to beware of approaching predators, and to change direction.

Sea horses tell of their love by clicking shyly, while the boatswain fish lives up to its name, playing a loud tune to its mate. If another suitor approaches, the tune quickly changes to a bellicose grunt, and the intruder is chased with a hail of piscatorial profanity.

Some fish have teeth imprinted with grooves, like those of a phonograph record. When they rub a certain tooth across the grooves, a special sound is produced. Many fish produce their sounds by drumming on their swim-bladders using special muscles and ligaments.

Tuning In

Frogs have only three main things to worry about: enemies, food and sex. The frog's hearing system reflects these concerns by allowing it to hear only the noises of its enemies or the sounds of a potential mate; food is located by sight. Any other noises are irrelevant to the life of the frog, and it cannot hear them.

Cricket frogs in the northeastern United States croak at 3,500 hertz, and the female can hear only mating calls in that frequency. Cricket frogs in parts of the Midwest croak at 2,900 hertz. An East Coast female cricket frog placed in that environment soon becomes an old maid, since she cannot hear mating calls below 3,500 hertz.

The coqui frog of Puerto Rico is named after the sound of its croak. The male emits the first half on a frequency heard only by other male coquis, announcing ownership of his turf—a warning to competitors. The second half is a mating call out of the range of male coqui frogs' hearing but clearly audible to the female. Both male and female coqui frogs have another frequency believed to be reserved for their enemies.

Good Vibrations

The built-in motion detectors of certain animals and insects are so uncanny that the term *supernatural* comes to mind. The cockroach can detect movements as slight as 2,000 times the diameter of a hydrogen atom. Pupae of cat fleas lie dormant in carpets for months, even years, until a human or a cat passes; then they spring into action. Stimulated by the vibrations of the intruder's movements and guided by body heat and carbon dioxide in the passerby's breath, they affix themselves to the body and begin feeding. A leaf-cutter ant buried in a cave-in taps a signal of distress on the walls of its prison that is heard over 5 centimeters away by worker ants, who rush to the rescue. Scout termites who hear an intruder approaching beat a warning message on the walls of their tunnel and enable other worker termites to scurry to safety. African mole-rats bang their flat heads against the walls of their burrows to identify themselves to other rats, to advertise their availability to a prospective mate, or simply to stake out their territory.

Each species has its own rhythms. Female brown planthoppers beat their abdomen against a leaf surface twenty times a second when they want to mate. Males hearing the drumbeat respond by drumming twenty times faster than the female, and the syncopation continues until the lovers are united. Whirligig beetles have fascinated generations of children by their ability to skate on a still pond without breaking the tension of the water surface. Even more remarkable is how swarms of the tiny bugs manage to race around a pond's surface and never collide with each other. Each beetle detects vibrations with a fine antenna that rests on the surface of the pond like a hockey stick and senses the ripples produced by other beetles, ignoring the ripples made by itself. The same system alerts the beetle to the approach of a predator or the arrival of a smaller insect suitable for lunch. The water-strider makes waves by beating the surface of the water and causing ripples that bounce back, signaling food. Water-striders announce their availability to the opposite sex by beating the water: ninety ripples a minute signals the presence of a male; ten ripples a minute, a female.

The Solo Duet
The most remarkable example of perfect timing in the animal world is the duet of the African bou-bou shrike. One bird will sing a note and then pause for two microseconds; during the pause the second bird picks up the tune, then pauses for two microseconds as the first bird resumes. So fast is this jungle duet that the human ear hears it as one, seemingly solo, song. Only when the song is recorded and played back at slow speeds does this remarkable timing become apparent.

Bird Songs
There are many types of bird songs, and it is believed that birds sing for several different reasons. A bird will sing some songs to advertise its presence in a given location and to notify other birds of that location. Certain other songs signal the bird's mate about some activity, and still others are performed purely for emotional reasons known only to the singer.

There is considerable variation in bird songs from species to species, and songs also vary depending on the season and the time of day. Some species, such as the warbler, will sing continuously throughout the daylight hours. The record for song performance is held by a red-eyed vireo, which is reported to have sung over 22,000 songs in a single day. It is said that the calls of the South American tinamöu, known as the "partridge of the Pampas," have such purity and softness of tone that they can be easily mistaken for the voice of a child. The songs of the tinamöu range from flutelike trills and whistles to rich organlike tones.

UNCOMMON
SCENTS

Trespassers Will Be Prosecuted

Animals would build fences if they knew how. The concept of sovereign territory is not an invention of man —it started with other animals. The roebuck, for example, stakes off its turf in March of each year. In an area containing woods and meadows, it paces off an enclosure varying from 25 to 250 acres, leaving on the trees and bushes a special scent secreted by a gland on its forehead. The roebuck goes along, rubbing its scent into various landmarks, making its rounds two or three times each day, because the scent evaporates after several hours.

During the winter months fierce battles are fought among the roebuck males for dominance, resulting in a division of the males according to who is the strongest. In March, however, when their antlers are covered with a tender and sensitive skin, the male roebucks cannot fight. The previous winter's battles have already established the rights and privileges of rank. If a lesser roebuck ventures into an area that has been marked off with the scent of one of his superiors, all it takes is a glance by the landholder to send the interloper fleeing for neutral territory.

The Smell of Success

The male African white or square-lipped rhinoceros is a tough customer who aggressively protects and patrols his turf, driving away competitors with savage fury. To make sure other male rhinos get the message, after he defecates he walks back and forth in the feces, stamping his feet to coat them generously. As he continues his patrol he deposits telltale odors around the landscape that warn other rhinos with territorial ambitions. The male hippopotamus, in order to stake out its territory, has evolved a special flattened tail, which he uses to flick back and forth vigorously to scatter his dung over a large area.

Many animals stake out territory with feces and urine. By leaving such calling cards the animal courteously introduces his territory, allowing the intruder to decide whether to challenge the claim or move to friendlier turf. This explains why city dogs are forever thoughtfully smelling the excrement of other dogs.

Some animals leave their scent along the path they travel which enables them to find their way back home. The bushbaby doesn't leave home without urinating on his hands. On the return trip he finds his way back by the odor of his urine. When an army ant stumbles upon a source of food for the colony, he runs back to spread the word, also spreading a special chemical on his way home.

Worker ants find their way to the cache by following this chemical trail. Ants travel long distances in single file using this trail; otherwise, they would soon lose their way. The chemical dissipates quickly, preventing future expeditions from following the old trail. Certain bees deposit their scent on the tips of plants along the route back to the hive. When the workers fly out to find the food, they follow this scent. When an intruder approaches a beehive, sentry bees attack and spray a warning chemical smelled by other bees, who come immediately to help. The same chemical alarm has the reverse effect when bees are threatened far from the hive, this time warning them to flee the scene and go home.

Leaving One's Mark

Dogs, when taken for a walk in a natural environment, will scrape their feet in the dirt after defecating. This is not to scatter the feces as a territorial marker, as it is with the rhinoceros or the hippopotamus. The only efficient sweat glands on a dog's body are between its toes, and the paw-scraping action serves to add another marker scent that establishes its presence in the area.

Why a Cat Rubs Your Legs

After a newcomer is examined visually by a cat, it approaches the stranger and, if it decides to be friendly, expresses this by rubbing its face and body back and forth against the legs of the new friend. While the cat is having its back rubbed, glands in its face deposit an identifying smell that help it recognize the newcomer next time. Wild cats, lions, and tigers are constantly rubbing each other, transferring the odor of the group, an activity that bonds them together and gives them a sense of security. A strange cat is easily identified by its alien odor.

Insect I.D.

Insect colonies generate a smell unique to each nest. A worker who has left the nest to go about its business is recognized upon its return by its smell. If it does not have the smell of that individual nest, even though it is of the same species, the insect will be killed instantly.

Amazingly, the colonies change the smell every day. If an insect is away more than 24 hours, it will return with the old smell to face immediate death.

COLORATION

An animal's coloring is closely related to its behavior and way of life. In the course of evolution, animals have developed the color patterns most appropriate to their respective niches, and, in particular, to the visual capabilities of other species in the community. For example, nocturnal animals usually are not brightly colored because the mechanism of color vision does not work well in low light conditions.

Coloration is most often adapted for either camouflage or conspicuousness. Camouflage has developed in many sophisticated ways as a means for an animal to hide from predators; conspicuous coloration may serve as a way to warn away predators, or it may provide an advantage in sexual competition.

Bird Coloration

Bird coloration performs useful functions. On the tip of a gull's lower beak is a red spot that serves as a bull's-eye when the hen is feeding her chicks, giving them a target at which to aim their open mouths. The kittiwake gull chick has a brown collar on the back of its neck, a signal the chick is helpless and doesn't want to fight. The quarrelsome kittiwakes are always squabbling and picking fights with each other. They make their nests on precarious ledges and in cracks in the faces of sheer cliffs. When a baby kittiwake is threatened it cannot run away, since there is no place to go, nor can it fly, because it doesn't yet know how. Instead the chick turns its face away from the aggressor, as if hiding from view. This act of abasement allows the other bird a full view of the brown collar, an unmistakable signal that the chick concedes the argument. Thus appeased, the soothed aggressor turns to other interests.

A Quick-change Artist

It is the chameleon's reputation for camouflage that is most puzzling. Chameleons can change to many colors, including dark green, light green, yellow, white, reddish brown, and brown. While these color changes disguise the animal, they are more likely to be used to reflect an emotional mood. Many chameleons change to brown when they are fighting, when green would be more appropriate—and safer—in their surroundings. The behavior and the quick signaling of their emotional state belies the label *cold-blooded*, used to describe these fascinating animals.

For years Americans have been buying what they thought were chameleons in pet stores, only to be disappointed when the tiny lizards didn't magically (as advertised) change colors to match their background. The normally bright-green lizard would occasionally turn brown and back to green, but nothing more. Thousands of lizards died of starvation when pet owners grew bored with them or simply didn't know how to feed them. The pet-store chameleons are green anoles from tropical America, related to the real chameleon but far less colorful. The real McCoys are usually larger, bizarre in appearance, and could serve as a model for a monster in a Godzilla epic.

The Jackson's chameleon resembles the dinosaur triceratops, with three "horns" pointing forward, an armor-plated head, and huge eyes that swivel in their sockets independently of each other. The chameleon can keep one eye on its prey on a lower tree branch while the other gazes behind it or watches the skies above for enemies. Its color-changing ability is only one of its remarkable features. Each of the chameleon's eyes is capable of moving 180 degrees in the horizontal plane and 90 degrees in the vertical one.

The animal has two toes on one side of each foot and three on the other, giving it a set of tongs grip a branch so tightly that only major force can pull it off. The grip is strengthened by a prehensile tail that coils around a branch like another arm, steadying the chameleon while it strikes at a target.

The chameleon's tongue is even more amazing. This organ can be extended to more than the length of the creature's body (in a large chameleon, as long as two feet) and ends in a rough club coated with glue that strikes the prey and brings it into the gaping mouth in a motion so fast it is sometimes impossible to see with the naked eye.

The chameleon's tongue is actually a long, hollow tube. When not in use the tube is compressed into tightly folded pleats within the creature's mouth. The chameleon will eat virtually any insect of reasonable size and is able to spot one from quite far away.

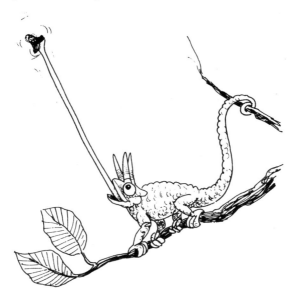

How Fish Talk

Semaphore flags and changes of costume are appropriate metaphors for communication among fish. Fish have limited but effective means of communication to show aggression, fear, and sexual readiness. Using their bodies as a slate, many fish can signal their intentions by turning themselves into flags of different colors that they can change to suit the needs of the moment.

The tilipia fish, of Southeast Asia and the east coast of Africa, turns a dark gray when it is ready to fight. If the opponent decides to concede the bout it shows the white flag by turning himself a ghostly white color as it retreats from battle. A pregnant female becomes dark silver. The courting male becomes darker and darker until he is matte black with blue stripes. As he becomes more desperate for a mate, his head will turn brown, his jaw white, and the tips of his fins a blood red.

The male stickleback of Europe turns three colors when mating or getting ready for battle. His topside becomes green, a long white stripe goes from head to tail along his side, and his underside turns crimson. When defending his turf he stands on his head, displaying his red belly to his antagonist, an unmistakable sign that a fight is imminent. The eleven-spined stickleback is usually green on top and silver-gray below. When ready for battle, he turns a deep black all over; when dressed for sex, he is black below and green above. Communication by color is common and widespread, serving as an almost universal language of the deep.

Seeing Red in the Deep Blue Sea

Mark Twain said that man is the only animal that blushes . . . or needs to. He didn't consider the octopus, which blushes bright pink when agitated or angry. The squid also turns bright red in a few seconds, and certain cuttlefish assume various colors and patterns to suit their emotions or needs. The common male European cuttlefish becomes a marine zebra when mating, turning himself into a black-and-white-striped billboard to advertise his availability to any amorously inclined female cuttlefish. Two huge, spectral black disks, resembling the eyes of a monster of the deep, appear on the back of a frightened cuttlefish, apparently to frighten away potential attackers. During this phase the rest of the cuttlefish assumes an ugly, mottled texture. When resting, the cuttlefish assumes a neutral color and a bland pattern.

Looking for a Fight

The hot-tempered male fiddler crab is always spoiling for a fight. He has a small pincer claw and a huge warrior claw longer than his body, which he waves menacingly when in danger or uses as a door to his burrow when resting. The way the crab carries this claw is reminiscent of a musician holding a fiddle. Depending on the mood of the moment, the fiddler turns his normally light-brown body bright red, purple, or black at will to reflect anger, sexual arousement, or fear. His color changes are not an attempt to camouflage himself. Instead they often make him stand out clearly in his environment, appearing to dare other fish.

BODY
LANGUAGE

The Lip-Flip Baboon
Baboons that are confronted by an enemy will draw up their upper eyelids to expose the light-colored skin surrounding their eyes, then flip their lips so that the upper lip covers their nose and the lower covers the chin. This both exposes their canine teeth and results in a grotesque and frightening face.

The Oldest Profession
The male hamadryas baboon is ready for sex at any time, whereas the female wants sex only when she is able to conceive. She signals her peak ovulation periods by a swollen and brightly colored sexual area at the base of her tail. When a female not in heat wants extra food or a favor from her lord and master, she approaches and shows him her posterior. A female hamadryas baboon's buttocks is a sight no full-blooded male baboon can resist. Copulation is immediate, and the cooperative female is granted various favors for her thoughtfulness and cooperation. So offensive was this behavior to the turn-of-the-century South Africa's Victorian sensibilities the government financed extermination campaigns against these "immoral" animals.

How to Keep Cats Away
Cats do not like being stared at by strangers; they consider direct staring a threatening behavior. If you wish to avoid any cat contact, simply stare fixedly at the cat with eyes wide open and make agitated hand movements beckoning the cat to sit in your lap. The only laps the cat will approach are those of unwary visitors who have quietly tried to avoid acknowledging its presence.

The Pecking Order

In the barnyard a rigid social order exists among chickens. In flocks of up to ten individuals, the cock is boss. After him, the hens peck each other until they are sorted out. At the top of the order are the stronger and most dominant; at the bottom the weakest, those who gave up in the pecking battles. Anyone who gets out of line is pecked at by her superiors, and often turns on those below it to show them who the boss is at this level. Alas for the hen at the end of the line; she gets pecked by everyone! The chickens recognize each other and know whom to push around and to whom to show deference. When placed in a strange flock, the chickens dropped their social order and simply fended as best they could.

ANIMAL COMMUNITIES

Just as there are names for groups of people gathering together, there are special words to indicate which animals are grouped together. Some of these words are heard all the time, such as *a flock of birds*. Other collective names are more unusual:

a colony of ants
a sleuth of bears
a swarm of bees
a herd or drove of cattle
a clowder or clutter of
    cats
a brood or clutch of
    chicks
a murder of crows
a brace or team of
    ducks

a tribe of goats
a band of gorillas
a down or hush of
    hares
a cast of hawks
a team of horses
a troop or mob of
    kangaroos
a leap of leopards
a pride of lions
a muster of peacocks

a gang of elk
a school or shoal of fish
a leash or skulk of foxes
a gaggle or flock of
  geese
a cloud or hoard of
  gnats

a bevy or covey of
  quail
a crash of
  rhinoceroses
a knot of toads
a pod or gang of
  whales

Large Colonies

While the North American badger is a hermit, his European cousins often tend to be communal. One badger colony in England has been inhabited for over 60,000 years.

Parrot Duets

Most birds are monogamous. In a few bird species such as swans and geese, partners are chosen for life and the couples often remain together throughout the year. Consider the parrot, whose entire social agenda revolves around the pair bond. Parrots mate for life, and in some species the parrot pair even complete each other's calls in a performance known as antiphonal dueting. One parrot begins the phrase, which its partner picks up in mid-arc and finishes. This is the parrot couple's way of assuring one another that all is well. When the two parrots are close together they sound like a single stereophonic bird. A parrot flock is really a collection of pairs that feed together, sleep together, and fly together.

One Matriarchy That Works

Recent research indicates that the elephant society is one of the most complex in the animal kingdom. Family bonds form the basis of enduring social relationships among elephants.

In the wild, elephants live in a matriarchal society that is usually controlled by the oldest and most dominant female. Her family is made up of her own daughters and granddaughters. Males leave the family at a relatively early age and either associate together or with an older bull. The old matriarch makes all the decisions for her family unit —including where they move, where they eat, and when they go for water—and she also maintains order and discipline. Baby elephants are taught at a tender age to respect their elders and to respond to the discipline of the family group. Since elephant mothers cannot continually watch over their youngsters, groups of infants are supervised and guarded by an older bull and cow. These babysitter elephants pre-chew food for the infants and ensure that none of them run off or wander away from the group. Babysitters also guard the young when they are asleep.

After long separations, bonded family groups may greet each other exuberantly. These mighty animals forget all decorum as they rush toward one another with heads raised high, rumbling, trumpeting, and flapping their ears. They actually spin with excitement and rub their massive bodies against one another, entwine their trunks, and click their tusks together.

When the matriarch of an elephant family dies, the effect can be extremely traumatic on the rest of the family. Survivors will mill around her body in panic. There can be total group disorganization, and sometimes families never recover.

Master Builders

The beaver has been around for 30 million years and is a rarity among mammals, because, like the reptiles, it never stops growing. Long celebrated for their ability to build dams, fell trees up to 3 feet in diameter, and construct underwater lodges that are safe havens for the female to brood in, beavers have another ability not as well known but equally mysterious and intriguing.

Beavers are master canal builders. They regularly build canals that often stretch to over 1,000 feet and are up to 2 feet wide and 2 feet deep. The canals serve as lumber flumes. The beaver floats logs and branches down the canals to the dam site for use in construction and also uses the canals to adjust the water level in the pond that forms behind the dam. Beavers have a very cooperative community. When danger is near, the beaver signals its family by slapping its broad tail on the surface of the water, sending warning sound waves into the underground den.

Jungle Dynasties

Life among the Hanuman langur monkeys of India has the makings of a television soap opera, should one ever be made about animal life. These simian societies produce situations replete with love, jealousy, fights for dominance, deception, manipulation, and murder. Each family group of twenty to thirty langurs has a male leader with exclusive mating rights to all the females. The male seeks to mate with as many females as he can, as quickly as possible, since the average leader has a reign of less than two years. He is constantly challenged by roving bands of bachelors seeking to take over the group and must continuously defend himself. If he loses a skirmish, he is exiled and spends the rest of his life as an outcast, alone and despised.

When a new leader takes over, he tries to murder the offspring of those females sired by his predecessor and then dominate the group with his own offspring. To counteract this infanticide the mothers develop an "auntie" network, passing their adored young from female to female. If push comes to shove, the females may face down the murderous male and chase him away. The mothers attempt to wean the babies quickly so they can go out on their own, leaving the mother free to mate with the new leader. The children resent this and throw temper tantrums, causing raucous treetop arguments. Conflict and a crisis every day are the staples of life among the langurs.

Teamwork

A lion will take advantage of opportunity and attack any prey that crosses its path. Lions do not have much stamina and are not able to keep up a long chase when trying to catch their prey. In order to ensure that enough food can be obtained to sustain its life, the lion has developed a routine that enables a pride to hunt cooperatively when necessary. The hunting group will split up into two subgroups. The first of these will charge a herd of prey and try to drive it towards the locations where the lions of the second subgroup lie in waiting. One of the waiting lions will run at top speed, attack the prey, and administer a fatal bite to the neck, by which time the other members of the pride will join in and devour the kill.

The Penguin's Burial Ground

The only common burial ground of animals that has ever been discovered belongs to the penguins of South Georgia Island in the Antarctic. A scientist from the American Museum of Natural History noticed after careful observation of the penguins' habitat that there were no dead birds to be found. One day as he explored a small clear lake at the top of a hill some distance from the ocean, he discovered several obviously sick or injured penguins drooping at the shoreline. Closer examination of the lake showed that its bottom was covered with dead penguins, the icy water having preserved their bodies in perfect condition. It appeared that the seriously ill and injured birds of the colony came to this spot to die.

MIGRATION

Flying by the Stars

Birds can read the skies and navigate by the stars. In a study, indigo buntings raised in captivity in rooms with no view of the sky and no natural light were brought into a planetarium and released. This was the first time in their lives that they had seen a "sky" or "stars," yet within minutes they had oriented themselves correctly, according to the migratory patterns of their species. When several stars were moved to false locations, the buntings became confused and disturbed.

In another experiment, a lesser whitethroat warbler born and raised in captivity was put in a planetarium set to a celestial location that would place it over Siberia instead of Germany, where the bird's migration normally starts. After several moments of indecision, the bird suddenly took off in a direction that would, if followed, correct the error and return it to its normal migratory pattern. Experiments under real skies confirmed the earlier tests, proving that maps of the stars and skies are somehow inherited as a genetic legacy at the moment of conception.

Feathered Olympians

If gold medals were awarded to species other than humans, migratory birds, insects, and many mammals would walk away with shelves of them. In the spring and fall, flocks of thousands of birds move from one region to another for feeding and nesting. Many birds travel for thousands of miles during the course of their migration. Over 100 million leave their northern homes every year to seek warmer climates. In a celebrated experiment to test the limits of the migratory instinct, sixteen albatrosses living on Midway Island were separated, taken thousands of miles apart, banded, and set free. Fourteen eventually found their way home despite being taken to places they normally would never see. Migrating birds have been recorded at heights of 20,000 feet.

The Arctic tern makes the longest migration of any bird. Arctic terns are born near the North Pole. When the young birds are old enough to travel, their parents take them to the South Pole. Two years later they are back at the North Pole again, having completed a round trip of 22,000 miles.

The ruby-throated hummingbird travels 500 miles nonstop across the Gulf of Mexico. The fuel expended by the bird weighs only .035 ounce, but it cheats a little by flying on a tail wind and gliding much of the way.

Whale Magnets

Whales cover thousands of miles in their annual migratory trips. How they manage to find their way across the trackless oceans has long been a mystery. Scientists now believe that the floor of the ocean is a vast road map of magnetic impulses used by whales to navigate around the globe. How the whales "read" this magnetic map remains unknown, but it may account for the occasional stranding of whales who run afoul of the magnetic system and go off course.

Butterfly Magnets

The monarch butterfly is the most famous insect traveler, fluttering yearly from central Mexico to Carmel, California, a daunting 2,500 miles. Butterflies that make the journey are descended several monarch generations from those who migrated the previous year. How do they know where to go and how do they arrive with such uncanny accuracy, even landing on specific trees occupied by their ancestors? Since the insects are several generations removed from their ancestors who migrated north the previous spring, the impulse to migrate has to be inherited. The butterfly's body contains minute quantities of the mineral magnetite, a material susceptible to electrical and magnetic forces. Scientists believe the monarch uses a combination of the position of the sun and the magnetic field of earth to find its way to California each year.

Smells of Home

After migration salmon return to their native river, where they spawn and then perish. The salmon are guided by their sense of smell and are able to distinguish the smell of the specific local water in which they were born and where they swam as small fry. If, at the fork of a stream, they head into water that does not carry the native scent, they let themselves drift downstream until they perceive it again and try an alternative course.

The Truth about Lemmings
The belief that lemmings blindly follow a leader who leads them to death off a high cliff or into the sea is, at least in part, wrong. What happens to these 4-inch-long Arctic European rodents is more akin to mass hysteria. At certain periods their population suddenly explodes. As they mill about in ever-increasing numbers, their activity level goes up and fights break out among the irritable, stressed animals, who run about aimlessly. The pressure is on. Soon a few at the edge of the crowd break out and start running to get away from the herd, and the rest follow in what is not a migration but a mob scene.

The lemmings don't know where they are going or why, but hundreds of thousands are frantically on their way. Soon they are totally out of control. Railroad trains have run over herds of fleeing lemmings, causing rivers of blood and mangled bodies. The irresistible rodent tide continues over the carnage, even running under the wheels of the moving train. Highways often have to be cleared to wash away the slippery blood. The fleeing lemmings will attack anything that gets in their way, barking like dogs. They snarl and leap at humans when in their frenzy and inflict painful bites. If they reach an immovable object such as a wall or cliff, the ones to the rear don't know what is happening and keep pushing, whereupon those in front plunge ahead; hence the mass suicide stories. If the lemmings reach the ocean, they plunge in and swim until they tire and drown or are eaten by predators, who quickly gather for the feast.

When lemmings are on the move, Eskimos come from miles around, not to catch them but to harvest the birds and animals who prey on them. Nature is never frivolous; this apparently insane animal behavior is possibly an evolutionary device to control the population by self-inflicted genocide. Fleeing for their lives, these normally shy rodents find only death.

The Strangest Migration of All

Salmon get a lot of credit for their amazing migration, but the one-way voyage of the eel is possibly the oddest journey in the world. The European freshwater yellow eel, after seven to fifteen years of lake or river life, suddenly changes from yellow to silver. Its eyes get larger and its snout gets pointier, as if nature streamlined it for a long trip. Soon the eel, a voracious eater, stops eating and is seized by a mission that will end its life. It finds its way to a river that leads to the ocean. If there is no river, it attempts to make its way unerringly to the ocean over land, through meadows, forests, and ditches, until it reaches rivers that will lead to the ocean. Once in the ocean the European eel heads straight for the Sargasso Sea in the Atlantic Ocean, a 4,000-mile trip that takes six months. After reaching the goal and mating, the adult male eels die. The hatched larva, an odd, semitransparent, leaflike creature, is able to make its way back to Europe without any guidance. After two to three years, during which they are growing, the larvae arrive at the end of their journey and another astounding change occurs: they stop feeding for a while; shed their baby teeth, which are replaced by new, larger, and sharper ones; lose their flat, leaflike structure, and become rounded. Then, by the millions, they travel up-river, where they will live out the rest of their lives until years later, when the call comes for the final migration of their generation.

Mammal Snorklers

Elephants can't jump off the ground; however, they are able to swim, in a way. An elephant will cross streams, rivers and lakes by walking on the bottom, and if the water is so deep that the elephant becomes totally submerged, the animal will raise its trunk above the waterline and use it as a snorkel.

PART THREE

Hunting
and
Hiding

ANIMALS SURVIVING

There are two things that are absolutely necessary for any animal to survive: it must be able to obtain food and to successfully avoid attacks from predators.

In order for any animal population to maintain its numbers over time, both of these critical survival prerequisites must approach perfection. Some of the most compelling facts about animals reflect their extraordinary solutions to the difficulties involved in hunting for food to eat and hiding from those who would eat them.

If an animal's methods of avoiding predation are not efficient, after a time the species will likely suffer extinction, since too few individuals will survive to mate and bear young. Conversely, those animals that feed on others must have the weapons and tactics necessary to ensure that they will have sufficient food, or they too will die out. The following examples represent a sampling of the variety and cleverness of the methods of survival and predation that have evolved in the animal kingdom.

World-Class Camouflage

When Claude Rains took off his bandages in *The Invisible Man*, he could go everywhere without being seen. He had the best camouflage in the world: invisibility. Certain animals have always had this ability and use it to hide from their enemies and find their prey. One-celled protozoans are transparent. When examined under a microscope the organs of these smallest of animals are seen as if in an X-ray. Some multicellular creatures such as the jellyfish, arrow worms, and other smaller forms of life appear to have X-ray organs as well.

As we move up the evolutionary scale to more highly developed creatures, invisibility becomes more complicated. Food eaten by invisible animals is visible in their stomachs, and the pigments required for the functioning of eyes are visible and would give away location. The Indian glass fish has a transparent body and gets around this inconvenience by concentrating the visible parts of its body in one spot—perhaps an imperfect solution, but an effective one. Certain fish have silvery scales that act like tiny mirrors, reflecting their surroundings and in effect making the fish as good as invisible.

Sloth Moss

The slow-moving three-toed sloth, which inhabits the upper levels of the tropical rain forest, grows green moss in its fur for camouflage. Its principal predator is the Harpie Eagle, which, despite its exceedingly sharp vision, has trouble seeing the moss-covered sloth against the background of green leaves.

Puzzle Picture

The spiny sea urchin, whose nutty meat is a delicacy in Japan, France, Chile, and other countries, is a quick-change artist, although a limited one when compared to its more talented ocean colleagues. This porcupine of the sea is normally a drab brown, the color of the muddy seascapes it inhabits. As the day wanes, the brown color begins to lighten and cool in hue until at night it is a pale, lovely shade of light blue.

The hands-down gold-medalist in coloration is a tiny prawn called the hippolyte, which becomes a transparent blue at night. The hippolyte has an enormous range of colors, which it uses to disguise itself, in chameleonlike fashion, depending on its surroundings. If it is on a bright green leaf, the hippolyte turns the same shade of green, purple, yellow, brown, or other color. Its versatility doesn't stop at mere color changes; the tiny creature also can adapt to the patterns of its background. If it is on a leaf, it mimics its veining and grain, and if the leaf has a pattern of algae or fungus growing on it, the hippolyte reproduces the random pattern of the growth until it becomes invisible. It is possible to gaze at an undersea scene inhabited by the hippolyte and its family and never be aware of their presence, so uncanny is their ability to camouflage themselves against any of the varied undersea backgrounds. In this way, the hippolyte has increased its chances of surviving in any environment.

The ability to change colors is widespread and highly developed among many undersea creatures. In a celebrated experiment a common flounder on a yellow, sandy background dutifully reproduced it in every detail until the fish was almost invisible. Then it was placed against a background consisting of multicolored pebbles. Again, the flounder not only copied the colors but also the random pattern of the pebbles. Finally, on a background of black-and-white checkerboard patterns the flounder's color/pattern processor presented a black-and-white pattern that approximated the checkerboard, a pattern never found in nature.

The Lights Fantastic

Many fish can generate light, which they use for a variety of purposes. The average light bulb dispenses 90 percent of electricity as heat and the rest as light, while fish who generate light waste only about 10 percent of the energy and convert the rest to light.

The hatchet fish and the viper fish have an array of lights on their undersides that are constantly adjusted to match the level of luminosity filtering through the water from the sky, making them invisible to predators below.

A Flashy Getaway

A luminous deep-sea shrimp, the Acanthephyra, follows the line of advice that "if you can't convince them, confuse them." When this creature is attacked it sets off a spectacular display of flashing lights that go off in blinding explosions, like flashbulbs on a camera. While the attacker is thus temporarily blinded and confused, the luminous shrimp makes good its escape.

Ink Spots

The cephalopods—the octopus, squid, and cuttlefish —have a devious device in their bag of tricks to confuse their attackers. They squirt a dark, inky fluid into the water, which surrounds the enemy. When the attacker blunders into the smoke screen, the cephalopod jets away by squirting water from its body. The inky coloring matter is valuable to artists, being the chief ingredient in the color sepia, named after the cuttlefish that secretes the fluid.

The Eel and the Octopus

The deadly moray eel likes nothing better to eat than a nice octopus. In the dark of night the eels emerge from their haunts and, using their keen sense of smell, begin to prowl for octopus. The octopus is not without its special defenses. As it flees from an approaching eel, it will squirt not ink, which is useless in the dark of night, but a special chemical that confuses the eel's sense of smell and throws it off the octopus' trail.

Borrowed Light

A species of deep-sea squid that cannot produce light by itself has solved the problem in an unusual way: it collects one-celled, luminous bacteria from the ocean and gives them a home in little sacs or tubes on its body, providing the glowing bacteria with a safe, comfortable environment. The squid sorts the bacteria by color, imparting a different luminescence to various parts of its body. The luminescent bacteria's rainbow colors help the squid attract a mate, locate prey, and identify itself to other approaching fish.

Squid that live near the surface squirt black ink at their enemies to confuse them while the squirter escapes. Because deep-sea squid live in a lightless environment, this defense is useless for them. Instead they squirt their light-producing bacteria at the enemy, dazzling it in a fog of blinding light. Relieved of its luminescence, the now-dark squid jets off into the protective darkness.

Don't Turn Your Back

When a skunk gets ready to discharge its malodorous secretion, it turns its back toward the object of its wrath, raises its tail, and stamps its front feet in warning. It seems the skunk is hesitant to discharge this fluid, because it smells so awful even to itself. If this warning isn't enough, the skunk lays down a barrage of odiferous spray that may be thrown ten feet or more with extreme accuracy. Only two or three drops may be expelled at once, yet it is so concentrated and powerful that it may be smelled for more than a mile in all directions.

The Musk Oxen Defense

When a herd of musk oxen is attacked by its worst enemies, arctic wolves and dogs, it forms a defensive circle with the young inside and the horned adults facing outward.

Why Cats Have Nine Lives

Cats are known to regularly survive falls from great heights that would kill any person. They inevitably fall by the hundreds every year in most major cities, given the abundance of high-rise buildings and the animal's tendency to fearlessly play with and chase other cats along ledges. Cats commonly survive plunges from six-story apartment buildings, and even those hurtling out of skyscrapers onto asphalt usually will not die. One cat is known to have survived a thirty-two-story plunge onto a sidewalk and suffered only a chipped tooth and mild chest injuries. Paradoxically, the higher the building is, the less risk a falling cat has of being killed. This ability to survive appalling drops is the main reason cats are said to have nine lives.

The secret to survival is the cat's ability to right its position while falling and then to spread out its limbs horizontally like a flying squirrel. It can thus increase its wind resistance and also decrease its terminal velocity and impact force. The impact is distributed over the whole body surface by the cat's perfect spread position at contact, rather than being concentrated on four legs or any single part of the body.

A Lizard with a Good Act

The horned lizard of North America does not bite and is easily gentled, but when threatened by man or beast this spiky creature will squirt a thin stream of blood from the corners of its eyes, hiss threateningly, puff up to a large size, and jump at its opponent. This spectacular performance usually works to scare off the threat.

Fluttering Eyes

One of the most effective deception techniques employed by an otherwise defenseless creature is the eyespot marking on the wings of the peacock butterfly. When resting, with its wings folded together above its body, the peacock butterfly is nearly impossible to see against a typical background. But when its wings suddenly flap open they reveal staring, colorful eyespots. These "eyes" discourage any bird that may be considering a meal. They are purely a bluffing device, since the butterfly would be helpless if a bird decided to attack.

Darwin suggested another reason these eyespots are lifesaving for the butterfly: they focus the attention of a bird or lizard to strike at or near them, thus protecting the more vulnerable organs of the butterfly. Even with part of a wing missing, the butterfly is able to escape.

Animal Actors

An oppossum will fall over and play dead when attacked. The sight of a poor, "dead" opossum is more than a healthy fox can stand, and it will usually skulk off, confused, its normal chase instinct disabled by the sight.

When the Alaskan rock sandpiper is disturbed in her nest she flies off, then suddenly drops to the ground dragging one wing helplessly and crying out in supposed pain. Sensing an easy kill, the predator stalks the "injured" sandpiper until the two are well out of range of the nest with its little chicks. Suddenly healed, the sandpiper takes off, no doubt laughing under its breath, leaving the frustrated predator a long way from the nest.

The harmless North American hog-nosed snake utilizes the fascinating animal defense of mimicry to scare off its predators. When disturbed, the hog-nose fills its lungs and hisses, and at the same time flattening its head and neck region by moving its back and ribs—exactly the same mechanism used by the deadly and much-feared cobra to spread its fearsome hood. If these warnings are not sufficient to dissuade a would-be predator, the hog-nosed snake will raise its head and strike, but it does not open its mouth.

This elaborate bluff is only one of this snake's defense mechanisms. If approached or touched, the hog-nosed snake will perform a very convincing play-dead act, rolling over on its back and lying limply with its mouth open and its tongue hanging out. Most predators do not like to eat dead snakes.

Why Cats Spit and Hiss

When a cat is confronted with a dangerous opponent or tormentor it invariably will perform a hissing-and-spitting display to ward off the danger. Although these sounds may not be very loud or ferocious, they are highly effective in frightening off a would-be attacker, even a very large dog. A little bit of intimidation often goes a long way.

A Regrettable Meal

The sea hedgehog can inflate itself like a balloon when in trouble, raising its sharp spines like a porcupine to ward off enemies. Sharks have occasionally swallowed these creatures, to their sorrow. In some instances the sea hedgehog has erected its spines inside the shark's stomach, giving the voracious killer a bad case of indigestion.

Does the Ostrich Bury Its Head in the Sand?

In a couple of words, sort of. If you were a bird that weighed almost three hundred pounds, stood eight feet tall, could not fly, and were being stalked by an enemy, what would you do? Ostriches can run 35 to 40 miles an hour, leaping along in 14-foot strides. Unfortunately, they generally run in large circles, making capture a simple matter. In such a fix, ostriches will often lie down and stretch their long necks straight out on the ground, trying to be inconspicuous. Stories of ostriches burying their heads possibly arose from travelers who saw them with their heads not readily visible and assumed the big birds had buried them.

The One-Footed Burrowing Shell

One very effective technique employed by numerous mollusks and other creatures is to burrow into sand or earth to disappear from the view of predators. The razor shell is one such mollusk that can vanish swiftly into the sand in case of emergency. Seven to 10 inches long, with a smooth, slender shell, it lies vertically in the sand. If it receives the slightest vibration through the sand—a disturbance that might indicate danger is approaching—the razor shell will burrow into the sand at an astonishing speed.

The foot of the razor shell mollusk is its unique digging tool. When retracted into and between the shell halves of the animal, the foot fills half the body cavity. When the mollusk needs to bury itself deeper in the sand, it protrudes its foot vertically downward. The pointed tip of the foot slices easily into the sand, and once fully extended it begins to swell as blood is pumped into it. The tip swells into a mushroom shape that serves as a firm anchor, and then the rest of the foot muscle is contracted, thus pulling the whole shell deeper into the sand. By pushing upwards on the swollen foot, the razor shell can resurface rapidly.

So That Others May Live

When a predator eats one fish from a large school of fish, how does the entire school know about it almost immediately and flee the scene? It turns out that certain species of fish have a chemical-alarm substance in their skin that is released only if the skin is broken—such as by the bite of a predator.

A scientist once was watching a group of immature minnows when a larger minnow arrived and immediately ate one of the small fry. Instead of fleeing when the alarm substance was released, the small minnows remained placidly in place, while the predator suddenly became extremely agitated and left the scene as fast as it could. Minnows do not develop their sensitivity to the alarm substance until they are a month or two old. The predatory minnow was mature enough to be sensitive to the chemical and when it ate the small fry the alarm substance was released, terrifying the predator and giving it an irresistible urge to flee.

Navigating by Memory

At high tide the frill-finned goby swims about, observing and memorizing every aspect of the small seascape among the tidewaters. As the tide ebbs, the goby is left to its devices while the ocean retreats. Using the memorized information, the goby leaps from puddle to pool and finds its way back to deep water with little trouble.

This ability to remember landmarks (or sea marks) is unusual for a fish but is common in most birds and mammals. Once a place has been memorized an animal will react automatically to what it knows is there, so it will be prepared when danger strikes. This can have amusing results when a landmark memorized by an animal is altered: the animal will continue to dodge nonexistent trees or leap over filled holes.

ANIMAL PREDATORS

The intricate and extensive web of animal life exhibits millions of creatures living together harmoniously, attacking one another only out of the necessity to eat. Predation is nature's way of controlling animal populations and assuring future generations that only the fittest animals will survive. The degrees of specialization of animal predation provide examples of just how selective an animal is in its choice of food. Certain animals will attack only certain specific other animals under certain specific conditions— and always, we believe, without actual malice or animosity. Even the much-maligned shark, who has managed to survive in the seas for 400 million years, is actually very meek. Under normal conditions a shark will attack only specific fish of a certain size and only when hungry. Sharks kill to eat, not to cause harm. Animal killings by other animals are never gratuitous; they always serve the purpose of survival.

How to Raise a Fighter
Unlike other mothers who bring dead food to their

young, the mother grizzly bear takes her hungry babies to the live food and teaches them to kill.

The Giraffe's Disadvantage

The giraffe's main enemy, the lion, will lie in wait to attack it while it drinks water. When drinking, with its legs spread awkwardly apart in a stiff and clumsy manner, it is unable to flee from the swift and hungry lion.

An Aquatic Can Opener

The use of tools is a sign of higher thought. Certain apes siphon ants out of anthills using a hollow straw. The sea otter is another clever and amusing tool user. Diving to depths of over 300 feet, the otter emerges triumphantly with a clam or abalone in one paw and a large rock in the other. Floating on its back it places the rock on its chest, steadying it with one paw, and begins smashing the clam against it with the other until it cracks open. Otters eat up to one-third of their body weight each day.

Watch Out

The female net casting spider is a great weaver; she doesn't sit around like the males of her species and wait for her prey to come along and get caught in her web. Instead, she weaves her strong web and then drops it on unsuspecting insect prey like a net.

Tongue-tied Insect Prey

The fastest tongue in nature belongs to one of the slowest-moving creatures in the animal kingdom: the amazing chameleon. Only after the invention of high-speed photography were scientists able to see how the chameleon uses its amazingly long and flexible tongue to catch insects. Lying in wait patiently for countless hours and changing colors with its environment to appear invisible, upon spying its prey it will slowly move to face its potential victim. Then, so slowly that the insect is not alerted, the chameleon's mouth opens slightly, giving the impression that it is merely yawning. A human observer's unaided eye will see only a tongue suddenly withdrawn and the jaws snapping shut, as though the chamelon had decided the insect was too far away to be captured. But the insect has unaccountably disappeared, and the chameleon is actually chewing and swallowing while its eyes are already scanning its surroundings looking for further unsuspecting victims.

On careful inspection of high-speed photos, we see the sticky globular tip of the chameleon's tongue—longer than the length of its own body—"fired" at the prey by a sudden muscular contraction. The full length of the tongue shoots out of the mouth at an incredible speed to capture the prey. The accuracy of the fired tongue is extraordinary, for if it were extended a tiny fraction of an inch too far or too little, the insect would be missed and would escape.

Fish That Use Bait

The angler is found in tropical and temperate waters throughout the world. It spends most of its time partially buried in the mud or sand on the bottom. The angler has something resembling a fishing rod sticking straight out from its head, at the end of which is the bait: a fleshy knot that dangles from the fish's upper lip directly in front of its open mouth, which acts as a tiny lantern. This bait glows in the darkness of the deep sea, its tantalizing luminosity provided by bacteria that live symbiotically inside it. This dangling, glowing knot wriggles in the current while the angler remains motionless. When its prey comes to investigate, the angler opens its mouth and the hapless prey is engulfed and swallowed fast. The fish has teeth that point inward in order to prevent its prey from escaping.

Other fish have developed their own special lures to help them attract their prey. The reddish frogfish dangles bait that resembles a wriggling worm, and the phynelox fish uses pink bait that coils and uncoils like a worm in the water.

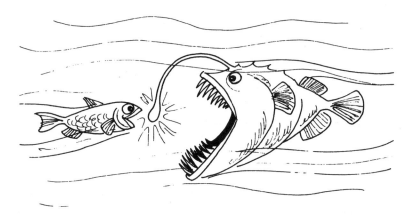

There's One Born Every Minute

"This way to the great Egress," read a sign in P.T. Barnum's circus. When the unsuspecting customers had passed through the doors, they found to their dismay that they were out in the street.

A similar but far deadlier fate awaits the naive fish who venture into the light show of the Chauliodus, a deep-sea viper fish. This fish has lined its mouth with 350 lights, of varying colors. When it opens its mouth, the interior light show is a splendid spectacle, irresistible to the little fish who flock in to see it. Once they are inside the viper fish shuts its mouth and swallows, ending the show.

Ships Passing in the Night

Thousands of feet below the surface of the ocean, where no light from above the water can reach, there exists an incredible nonstop luminous display. Many fish have the ability to shine their own lights in displays that serve as a visual language. The primary use of these underwater light shows is identification. Each illuminated fish has its own peculiar arrangement of lights, whose placement, sizes, colors, and brightness vary not only from species to species but from male to female within a species. A fish can tell whether an approaching illuminated fish is friend or foe, mate or meal, by recognizing the specific arrangement of lights.

The untouchable bathysphere fish has twenty light-blue "portholes" running along each side of its body, giving the fish an uncanny resemblance to a passing passenger ship. A 3-foot-long tentacle hangs from its lower jaw and another from its tail, each with an illuminated lantern—the front red and the rear blue—at the end. These are not a ship's running lights, but rather fishing rods designed to attract unwary prey. When an unsuspecting fish comes to investigate, the bathysphere springs to life and tears the prey apart with needle-sharp glowing teeth that are lit from within.

A Searchlight in the Sea

A fantastic fish named pachystomias goes hunting with a searchlight. The pachystomias emits a powerful beam of red light that it alone can see. It sweeps the dark sea with this floodlight, in search of prey. Since other fish cannot see the red portion of the spectrum, they are unaware of the searchlight shining on them. Once Pachystomias has a meal in sight, it locks his beam onto the unsuspecting prey until it is close enough to gobble it.

Big Mouth

The deep-sea perch is known as the great swallower. Its enormous jaws enable it to eat fish twice its size. The perch's inward curving teeth prevent a fish, once captured, from wiggling free and backing out, and its stomach is able to expand to accommodate the oversize dinners.

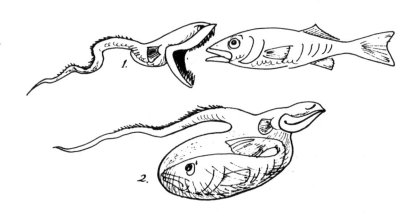

The Tasmanian Devil

The Tasmanian devil has earned a reputation for ferocity. Its ears turn bright red when it is aroused, projecting a clear warning of what is coming next. A meat eater, the devil is the size of a badger and has the face of a bear. Unlike the kangaroo, its pouch opens to the rear, a logical arrangement for a four-footed beast that runs around in the underbrush. The rumble-seat format prevents sticks and rocks from entering the pouch during the mother's travels. The devil is a strong animal with huge teeth and a snarling scream calculated to frighten any foe. Despite its aggressiveness, the poor devil is near extinction.

The Deadly Diversion

We're told that a rattlesnake's rattle is for warning us away—seemingly thoughtful behavior on the snake's part—so we do not disturb the snake. Charles Darwin taught that one species would not have developed a trait solely for the good, or survival, of another, so there must be another reason for the warning. Scientists now believe that the rattle is not a warning at all but the rattler's way of diverting attention to the wrong end of the snake. As the prey looks at and listens to the rattle its concentration breaks for a few seconds, long enough for the rattler to strike. The rattle acts as a ploy, a little diversion to unbalance the prey, giving the rattler a moment of confusion to do its work.

Hide That Nose

The polar bear feeds primarily on the ringed seal. Its eyesight and sense of smell are both very acute, and it can identify a seal's den from quite a distance. The bear approaches stealthily with its head lowered and will instantly flatten itself on the ice if the seal raises its head, even cradling its face in its paws in order to hide. Polar bears have been known to push a small block of ice in front of them while stalking seals, perhaps in order to hide their black noses.

Riders of the Purple Reef
Undersea cowboys ride their mounts in the clear waters of the Red Sea off the coast of Israel. The trumpetfish climbs aboard a passing parrotfish, hiding itself so cleverly that it is unseen by its prey, who allow the harmless larger, vegetarian fish to come close to them. When they are within striking distance the trumpetfish springs from ambush and gobbles the unsuspecting prey, then returns to its docile mount to continue the patrol. Some species of trumpetfish have further developed their specialization by changing color and pattern to match that of their mount.

Don't Badger Me
The grouchy badger will stand its ground when attacked —even by animals larger, heavier, and more menacing. The badger relies on its formidable teeth and strong jaws; its remarkably long claws, used to burrow into the ground; and a loose-fitting hide that makes it appear larger than it really is. When a predator grabs a badger by the scruff of

its neck—a usual approach—the badger has so much room in its loose skin that it turns around inside the skin and attacks the predator from below, usually the most vulnerable spot.

A badger will eat anything that crosses its path, including a poisonous snake, which it kills, after which it carefully decapitates the venomous head and eats the carcass. Badgers especially love to eat bees, whose stinging has no effect on the loose, tough hide of the attacker.

A Snake in the Grass
Many animals are picky eaters and search out specific foods for their diet. The African egg-eating snake feeds exclusively on eggs, robbing bird's nests and chicken coops. Set far back inside the snake's mouth are throat teeth, whose purpose is to crack the shell of an egg when the snake has stuffed it far enough back to be within their reach. When the contents of the egg are swallowed, the egg-eater vomits out the shells.

Where the Stars Dine
The starfish, a particularly odd animal, has been around for a long time. Watching a starfish on the prowl requires patience. It slowly creeps along, seemingly going no place, then suddenly stops, almost as if it were thinking. It has smelled a clam buried four to six inches below in the sand.

Slowly the starfish begins shoving the sand aside, using its arms. Some time later a hole over two feet in diameter has been dug, revealing a juicy clam in the exact center. The starfish mounts the helpless clam and wraps its thick arms about it. When it is in position it pulls the clam shells apart with incredible brute force. Once the clam is on the half shell and ready to be eaten, the starfish's stomach emerges from its mouth, covers the meat, and begins to digest it. Once the starfish is finished with its meal, its stomach retracts into the body and this strange creature begins its search for another clam.

Taking Aim

The archerfish spits its prey to death. Lurking just beneath the surface of the water, it waits until an insect alights on a twig above it. Taking aim, it corrects for the refraction of light in the water and lets fly. The drop of water speeds unerringly and knocks the insect off his perch, into the waiting mouth of the predator. The archerfish, which may grow as long as nine inches, is able to shoot the water by closing its gill flaps so rapidly that the water in its mouth is expelled. Its marksmanship is usually quite accurate up to three feet away. It can also release a volley of up to five or six shots in fairly rapid succession if it fails to hit the target with its first shot.

A High-Speed Life

The tiny elephant shrew, named for its long nose, is a very busy animal in its native African homeland. The shrew stakes out an extensive territory and manages to memorize every step of the paths through its domain. Using these predetermined paths when out hunting for prey, it not only follows the same general route but places its feet in exactly the same spot each time it makes its rounds. The elephant shrew will have identified various holes and rocks as safe places to hide in if attacked, and it performs a drill as it passes each one, popping into a hole or behind a rock for a few seconds before hurrying onward.

Once the territory has been determined the shrew will hunt continuously, day and night, improving the odds that food will be found. As it leaps along it gulps down insects on the wing, stores them in its cheeks, and chews them while still running. The shrew is so quick at securing its insect prey that the procedure is difficult to see with the unaided human eye.

Fast Food
The cheetah may be capable of reaching speeds of 70 miles per hour, at least for very brief periods, and is known as the world's fastest mammal. It uses this terrific speed in order to catch its prey; however, it can sustain top speed only for a distance of a few hundred yards. It then takes the cheetah up to fifteen minutes to catch its breath before it can make another dash. The cheetah is very particular about its food. It does not eat any of the internal organs except for the liver.

Nasty Fish
The slime eel, also known as the hagfish, is a repulsive creature about a foot long with no jaw and no bones. The half-blind horror feeds on dead or dying fishes and will enter through the anus or the mouth and eat the fish from the inside, leaving nothing behind but skin and bones. The hagfish can secrete enormous quantities of slimy mucus

from glands located all over its body and from special slime glands along its sides. Among its other physiological features, it has four sets of hearts at different places in the body to keep its low-pressure blood flowing. A hagfish is born with both testes and ovaries and may produce sperm one season and eggs the next.

The Rodeo Spider

The common bolas spider uses a lasso to capture its favorite food, a moth in flight. Hanging several inches below a twig by a silken-threaded "trapeze-line," the bolas spider draws out a second line and attaches droplets of sticky silk to it. The spider uses its hind legs to comb the droplets downward until they form a single large globule at the end of the line. This line will then be used to lasso a passing moth attracted by the scent of the silk globule. Poised in the middle of its trapeze-line, the spider holds the bolas-line with one of its exceptionally long front legs and waits. At precisely the right moment the spider tosses its lasso at the passing moth, attaching the sticky end to the moth's underside. The victim is halted in' midflight, and the spider descends the bolas line to kill the moth with one poison bite of its jaws.

The spider then proceeds to wrap its prey in silk and to suck out the body juices of the moth at leisure. When its meal is finished, it cuts the trapeze-line so that the dried remnants of its prey fall to the ground.

One hypothesis for the incredible accuracy of the bolas spider's lasso is that the spider can detect the vibrations of an insect's wings through the suspended threads of its trapeze-line.

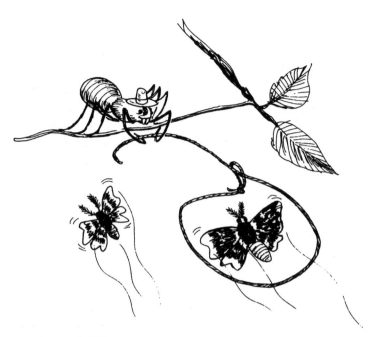

Sound Blasts

After potential prey has been discovered by echolocation the dolphin steps up the volume of its sound bursts, aiming directly at the fish or school of fish. When the sound waves hit, the fish are stunned and become disoriented, making it a simple matter for the dolphin to scoop them up. Sperm whales can generate sound beams from their heads of up to 265 decibels, enough to stun large fish and kill smaller ones on impact. By comparison, the sound from a jet aircraft at takeoff heard from a distance of 100 feet is 145 decibels.

The pistol shrimp holds its deadly claw open with two suction cups. When it attacks it closes the claw, pulling the suction cups apart with a pop so loud it can be heard a mile away. The noise confuses the prey. When the shrimp grabs it in its other claw it administers the coup de grace by firing its pistol a few more times, killing the prey.

Stunning Fish

Pliny the Elder recorded the shocking news of the discovery of the electric ray in the first century, calling it the numbfish. The ray generates a 90-volt current, enough to stun any food fish in the vicinity. Once a fish receives a shock the ray waggles its body, creating an undertow that sucks the stunned fish into its waiting mouth, then settles back in the muck to digest its meal and await the next customer.

The electric eel is the one to watch out for. This fish dedicates half its body to the production of electricity. It can unleash a lethal 550 volts, enough to kill a human and more than enough to finish off most fish unlucky enough to feel the sting. The electric eel is found only in rivers in northern South America, usually among dense vegetation in shallow water. It is not a true eel but a fish, a distant relative of the carp, minnow, and goldfish. Approximately

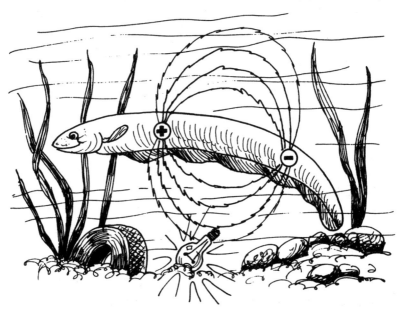

four-fifths of its length and 40 percent of its body weight is composed of the highly specialized organs used to generate electricity. An adult electric eel can produce paralyzing discharges exceeding 600 volts, enough to light a neon bulb or kill most other fish. The eels can perform this astonishing feat 40 times a second. It is not necessary for the eel to actually touch its victims, since the shocks create a strong electric field for several feet around it. It is capable of precise and measured discharges of voltage depending on whether it is exploring, mating, or stunning and killing prey. The all-important tail of the electric eel will grow back quite quickly if lost or removed. Its stunning abilities leave it with no natural enemies and a long lifespan.

Electric fishes living in the sea, such as the electric ray, do not need to produce voltages as high as does the electric eel, since sea water has a much lower resistance to electricity than does fresh water. Instead, the electric ray produces a very high current, so that at only about 50 volts the power output may be as much as 6 kilowatts.

POISONS

The Spitting Cobra
The spitting cobras of Africa and Asia squirt venom accurately from 6 feet away using special mouth muscles surrounding the venom sacs. The snake blinds its enemy and gets away in the confusion. The blinding venom is extremely painful. The antidote is an immediate rinse with milk, which neutralizes the venom.

The Poison Arrow Frog
The most poisonous creature in the world is the Amazonian yellow frog called the kokoi, also known as the poison arrow frog. The Amazonian Indians use poison

from the skin of these frogs to tip their instantly lethal arrows. The yellow frog's deadly surface is so poisonous that one cannot touch it without suffering serious ill effects. Only one hundred thousandth of a gram (0.0000004 ounce) of the poison can kill a man.

Poison Spurs

The duck-billed platypus is one of the oddest creatures in nature's bestiary, with wondrous features. Among the male platypus' repertoire is the ability to inject a poisonous venom in an enemy. He does this with a hollow spur located on each ankle, connected to a gland in the leg that produces the poison. The platypus injects the venom by spurring an enemy with his leg. Although not fatal to humans, the venom causes excruciating pain and suffering for months until it dissipates from the system. Other platypuses and animals they attack will often die from the effects.

The only other venomous mammal is the shrew, notably the short-tailed shrew of North America, which produces a poisonous saliva that can be introduced into the wound when the creature bites its victim. It uses the venom to disable mice and other small animals. This venom is also unusually painful, although not fatal, to humans.

PART FOUR

Making
More
Animals

ANIMALS COURTING

All animals, if their species is to survive, must have an efficient means of reproducing their kind, often amidst the most extreme and adverse conditions known on earth. The extraordinary variety of effective solutions invented by nature to perpetuate animal species includes perhaps the most astonishing of all the phenomena in the animal kingdom. There are strategies for successful mating that seem quite strange on first inspection, yet their beauty and simplicity inspire awe. The ways in which animals meet and greet each other, seduce each other, and perform the mating act are nearly limitless. Whether underwater, on land, or in the air, somehow animals find a way to mate and reproduce. It is as if some great playwright or poet imagined every possible scenario for seduction and sex and then invented animal players to walk (or swim or fly) the stage.

Male or Female?
Among higher animals choosing one's gender is rare, being known only in one family of turtles and one of

alligators. It is more common among lower forms such as fish and worms. We are not talking about males or females pretending to be of the opposite sex but of them becoming the gender they want to be, complete to the physiology.

The silverside, a small fish of the Atlantic, decides what sex to be based on the temperature of the water at the time. If cold, it develops as a female; if warm, a male. It is desirable for females to be born earlier in the season, when the water is cold, so they have enough time to grow large and can carry many eggs. Size is not important for the male, because all he has to do is produce sperm; therefore a shorter growth period, resulting in shorter males, works best. Early concentration on female births means there will be plenty of them around for the males to fertilize. An excess of males or a shortage of females could lead to disaster. Silverside fry raised in laboratories at temperatures between 52 and 66 degrees Fahrenheit produce twice as many females as those raised in water between 63 and 77 degrees.

The bonellia, a sea worm, chooses its sex depending on what happens to the rest of the worms. During its early development if it finds itself in a group with a lot of male bonellia, it becomes a female, and vice-versa. The difference is marked, since the male remains a microscopic blip while the female develops into a mature worm one inch long. To ensure that he is Johnny-on-the-spot when needed, the male bonellia makes his home in the genital tract of the female.

Alligators usually lay from twenty to fifty eggs, which are guarded by the mother. An odd feature about alligator reproduction is that the incubation temperature of the eggs determines the sex ratio of the offspring. Experiments have shown that low nest temperatures produce only females, whereas high temperatures produce only males.

It's a Female's World

Because male wood rats mate with several females, it takes fewer males to continue the population. For the good of the species it is better to have a few males mating with many females than many males fighting over a few females. When things are going fine for wood rats, nothing much happens. When food is scarce and the rats begin to starve, a strange phenomenon occurs: the mother rat begins to favor female babies and reject males. If conditions are sufficiently harsh, the male baby rats will die as the indifferent mother continues favoring his sisters. Population control and family planning is often thought to be a function of humans only, yet the little wood rat controls the population of its species, ensuring survival and balance.

Trouble in Paradise

A chilling analogy for us "higher types" may be implied from a remarkable experiment by a biologist at the National Institute of Mental Health. The scientist released four pairs of mice into mouse heaven: a room containing all the nesting material, food, and drink the mice could ever need. Absent were any natural predators or pressures of daily life; all the fortunate mice had to do was enjoy themselves. They immediately devoted themselves solely to sex and eating. Five hundred sixty days later there were 2,200 mice in the room, the peak population of this little love nest. Four years later, all the mice were dead. They had lost the will to live. Their sex drives had disappeared, along with normal behavior patterns of the wild that delineate the sexes. The declining days of the rodent hedonists were spent grooming their bodies, eating, and sleeping. Their social instincts had declined along with everything else, although the amount of food and drink they consumed was constant.

The Fittest Kittens

The dasyure is fond of hunting mice and birds and is about the size of a domestic cat. There the resemblance ends, since the dasyure is actually a marsupial. This creature is a unique example of the survival of the fittest. The female has six teats yet gives birth to a few dozen baby dasyures at a time, each a half-inch long or less. The first six that get to the teats are secure; the rest will die. When the lucky half-dozen outgrow the pouch they continue to hang on to the mother's fur as she goes about her hunting, becoming an increasingly heavy burden for her.

Population Control at the Frog Pond

If a large tadpole is put into a tank containing younger tadpoles, the small ones soon become despondent, refuse to eat, and eventually die. Even when only the water in which the larger tadpole had been swimming is poured into the tank, not the tadpole itself, the little ones have the same reaction.

If too many tadpoles are born into a small pond, they will quickly use up the available food supply and mass starvation will follow. By the secretion of a chemical substance that causes the younger, less-developed tadpoles to die and leaves the bigger, stronger ones to develop into mature frogs, the entire frog population of the pond is regulated. The chemical is nature's way of ensuring that the frog pond will remain in balance and that there will always be enough food, and room, for new frogs.

Starting Young

Amphibians, such as frogs, toads, newts, and salamanders, live in water and on land. When in water amphibians are able to obtain oxygen via the skin, whereas on land they breathe air into their lungs. Most amphibians begin life in the water and later undergo a metamorphosis that fundamentally changes their body structure from the larval stage of development into a mature adult form. Although most species cannot reproduce until they have reached adulthood, some salamanders are able to reproduce while still in the larval stage of development, a type of reproduction called neotony.

FINDING
MATES

Mr. Wren Builds His Dream House

Architect Sir Christopher Wren's feathered namesakes are also architects, if not as famous for their designs. The English wren begins building a nest before he has a mate. Not satisfied, he abandons it and starts another one in a different site. Still not satisfied, he abandons the second and begins a third. Learning his trade by trial and error, the wren finally gets the nest right, and it is a thing of beauty. He builds it from spider's webs, grass, lichens, moss, and hairs and lines the bottom with feathers. Then he puts a nice roof over the nest and makes a hole just big enough to fit through. Ready to settle down, the male ventures out, advertising his model home until he finds an interested female, whom he takes on an inspection trip to the site. Strutting ahead, he preens himself and coos sweet nothings as the female shyly follows behind, feigning indifference. At the site he shows her excitedly around the manse. If she likes what she sees, the deal is concluded and the two settle in for some serious billing and cooing.

The Mansion of Birdland

The house-building skills of the wren are impressive, but they cannot come close to those of the satin bower bird of Australia, an animal with a keen aesthetic sense. After selecting a site the male bower bird spends several weeks building the outer walls with twigs and leaves, which he carefully arranges so they come together overhead. Then the hard work begins. Flying long distances, the bird scouts the riverbanks for pretty stones, shells, bleached bones of small animals, and even the skulls of mice and other birds. Laboriously lugging these treasures back to the nest, he artfully places them around the base of the walls and makes little paths into the nest with them. Bower birds living near cities will fill their nests with *art trouvé*: bottle caps, clothespins, bits of colored glass and paper, or anything that attracts their artistic eye. They love the color blue and collect blue items to build into the nest. There are hundreds of stones and other items in a typical nest. Not content, the bird chews berries, smearing their colorful pulp around the bower in various designs. Finally he is ready for a mate. Eventually he entices a female to his new home, but after courtship and mating have taken place the nest is abandoned and a separate, very plain, nest is constructed for rearing the young.

Time For a Dentist

A tomcat with no teeth would have a difficult time trying to become a father, because he will have trouble clinging to the female's neck with his teeth while mating and therefore would likely not mount her successfully.

A Little Snack before Bed?

Tit-bitting, or tid-bitting, is a ruse used by some male birds to disarm the hen's shyness so he can have sex with her. The red jungle fowl's approach seeks to allay her qualms at his imposing appearance. The cock bends down and pecks at the ground in imitation of a mother hen's pecking, used to signal her chicks that food is near. The hens immediately go into a frenzy and mating quickly follows.

The Palawan peacock pheasant takes the ploy a step further and finds a grub or other snack to offer to the hen. As she nibbles shyly at the snack he struts regally around her, surveying his latest about-to-be conquest.

The peacock ritualizes the procedure to an abstraction. Approaching the female with his famous fan spread in all its iridescent glory he bows formally, allowing an unobstructed view of his magnificent tail, a rainbow of colors unmatched in the animal kingdom. It is a sexual flag for the female, so the bow that precedes it—an echo of the ground pecking that accompanied the hen's early feeding —is a symbol that good things are on the way, as well as a method of making his intentions perfectly clear by getting his body out of the way so that only the tail dominates her view.

Perfumes and Aphrodisiacs

During courtship a brush appears at the end of the male queen butterfly's body that gently dispenses a fine, scaly dust over the female flying below him. She is transfixed by the odor, and mating begins. The male does not manufacture the magic elixir but gets it from a certain plant. Certain moths release aphrodisiac perfumes from the ends of hollow hairs on their abdomen and then wave the potion over the female by fluttering their wings.

Sidling up to a female, the two-lined salamander bites his lady love and injects an aphrodisiac into her bloodstream through his hollow fangs, after which he can do with her what he will. The newt squirts his aphrodisiac into the water and then begins vibrating his tail at the fascinated female newt. The vibrations float the love potion over to her as she watches the display. During the mating season, the female red deer is in heat for only one day. Stags continually sniff her urine until the odor tells them she is ready. Camels drink the female's urine for the same purpose, swishing it around in their mouth as connoisseurs would a fine wine.

The Largest Harem

The male fur seal is known to average sixty wives at one time, and an exceptionally strong bull fur seal may have over one hundred mates. As the male seals arrive each spring at their breeding grounds in the Bering Sea near Alaska, each one appropriates a section of the beach for his future wives. When the females finally appear, the bull captures as many as he can and herds them to his selected spot on the beach. He then remains on guard for the months they are on land, fighting any other bull that approaches his territory and driving any wandering females back into his fold.

Ostrich Polygamy

The ostrich lays the largest egg of all birds; it weighs three pounds. It takes roughly two dozen hen's eggs to fill one ostrich egg. However, in proportion to its body size, the ostrich egg is the smallest of any bird's egg. The male ostrich is polygamous and will take several females at once as mates. They all make one large nest in the sand, and the females fill it with fifteen to twenty eggs. The male stands guard and incubates the eggs, protecting them from predators.

They're Playing Our Song

Even when the female canary is provided with a nest box and a suitable mate, her eggs do not begin to develop until she hears the one special melody that triggers the pituitary gland in her brain to release the hormones that start her breeding. Her ovary will ripen and the eggs develop faster the more the male canary sings to her.

How to Have a Safe Courtship

Shark courtship is a potentially lethal affair because of the often-ferocious nature of the encounter between male and female sharks. For this reason the male shark will cease to eat prior to breeding season, thereby reducing its vitality. Since the females do not undertake a similar fast, and since they are on the average larger than the males, it is often the male shark who is in greater danger.

The Eagle's Flight

During courtship, the golden eagle performs spectacular nuptial flights. The most amazing flight-skill display involves the male nosediving toward the female as she suddenly turns onto her back in midair so that the couple's claws will touch lightly.

A Strange Serenade

The male porcupine sings a high falsetto song to attract a partner. When the female approaches, the male rears up on his hind legs and prances forward, exposing his erect penis. If the female porcupine is in heat, she will approach the male, who then urinates on her before performing the sex act.

156

Behind the Wall

When the hornbills of Asia, India, and Africa are ready to start a family they shop for a hollow tree, in which the female lays two or three eggs. The male then brings mud to the site and he and his mate wall up the nest, with the female and the eggs inside. Mixing their droppings into the mud to make it stronger, they are finished when the opening is completely covered except for a tiny hole just big enough for the female to receive the food the male pokes through it. The male hornbill (named for the enormous beak) spends the next few weeks bringing home the bacon, stuffing tidbits of food through the hole to the waiting female.

When the eggs hatch the couple breaks through the hardened wall and the half-naked, bedraggled female, who has moulted while in the nest, emerges. Then the couple set to work and wall in the chicks, again leaving a small hole for food, until they are big enough to emerge permanently from the now foul-smelling, messy nest. All this is designed to prevent passing monkeys or snakes from helping themselves to a meal of baby hornbill.

A Fighting Fish Ritual

The male and female Indian fighting fish have an elaborate breeding ritual in which the eggs shed by the female are caught in the anal fins of the male and cradled gently as he fertilizes them. The male then releases the eggs, which float gently down through the water as the female quickly gathers them in her mouth. Once her mouth is filled with her fertilized eggs, she swims into position facing the male and spits them at him one by one; the male catches them and stores them in his mouth, where they will safely remain until hatching.

Elephant Courtship

A male elephant may pursue and court a female for up to three years before she acquiesces to mating. Elephants display great sentimentality and tenderness in their pair-bonding rituals. They use their trunks to caress one another and will walk together, trunk in trunk, as if holding hands.

During their courtship, the male will treat the female with many kindnesses, share food, and protect her.

Once a female elephant has chosen her partner, she will refuse the advances of all others. She will, in fact be faithful for about three years—throughout the period of gestation and for many months after the birth of her baby.

Elephants prefer privacy for the love-act; they will seek out woods and secret places behind huge rocks or trees or in caves. Oftentimes the huge creatures will prefer to mate in water so that the male's weight, while mounting the female, can be more easily supported. The male will mount the female with ease, tenderness, and grace, and remain there for only four or five minutes.

ANIMAL
SEX

On Their Own

Many simple animals contain glands of both sexes. They don't need a mate, because they can fertilize themselves. This is a necessity for permanently affixed sponges, semipermanently located mollusks, and free-drifting jellyfish, assuring the survival of the species by taking the element of chance out of the reproductive process. Slugs mutually fertilize each other. Placing themselves together, head to toe, one slug passes sperm to the other while the partner passes sperm to him/her/it.

The Odd Couple

A strange sexual union takes place in the pitch blackness of the suboceanic world a mile beneath the surface, where pressures are great and darkness intense. Living beings assume grotesque forms and behavior in the stygian gloom. The newly hatched, semitransparent, toothless, and vulnerable male anglerfish larva begins searching for a female to mate with before it becomes a mature fish. Eventually a female appears, comparable in size to the male as the Queen Mary to a tugboat. Well-equipped for her role as an aggressive food-gatherer, her formidable armor-plated exterior bristles with pointed appendages and sharp spines that would give any attacker pause.

Fearlessly, the tiny male swims up to the dreadnought. The female watches the approach with interest, recognizing this pipsqueak not as a delicious morsel but as a creature with a higher purpose, and one of her tribe. The male grabs the female's body in his mouth and fuses to it. He remains there as a parasite for the rest of his life. His heart continues to beat and gills bring oxygen into his system, but his eyes and mouth degenerate and become useless, since there is no further need for them. Up to four males will fasten themselves to an eligible female in this manner, all waiting for the big day. Soon the female ovulates. The discharge of eggs sends a signal to the male, who discharges his sperm, fertilizing the eggs. Then he slowly deteriorates, eventually falls away from the female and dies.

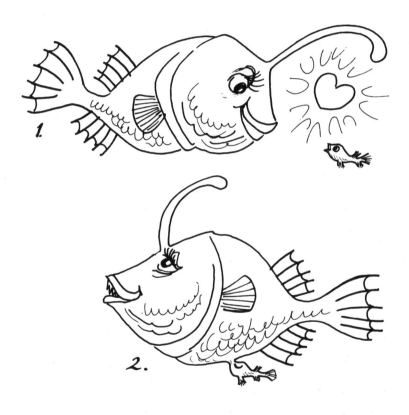

Most Efficient Mating Awards

After mating, the female dwarf top minnow is able to retain any unused spermatozoa in her ovary for up to a year and is thus able to fertilize successive batches of eggs with only one mating. This long retention of live sperm also makes it possible for two or more broods of minnows of different ages to be developing simultaneously in the ovary.

Several different mammal species are capable of delaying the implantation of the fertilized egg. Northern fur seals can keep a fertilized egg dormant for a full year. This delay helps to ensure that the babies are born at the proper time of the year, in some species so as not to interfere with annual migrations.

Spider Sex

Male web-spinning spiders will pluck out a signal on the main radii of their webs when ready to mate. The females will signal back their willingness (or their disinterest), and only when it is safe to do so will the male approach and mount his mate, for if she is not prepared for or responsive to mating, the female spider often will attack and kill the careless male. Cannibalism is a well-developed instinct in spiders.

If the mating is successful, the spermatazoa deposited into the female can remain alive almost indefinitely until a batch of eggs is laid; in fact, the spermatazoa obtained at a single mating are sufficient to fertilize any number of batches of eggs laid over many months or seasons.

Of Time, Tide, and Grunions

Each year hundreds of people go to Southern California beaches to watch (and catch) fish during the annual spring grunion run. Thousands of tiny male and female grunions wait offshore until high tide under the full moon from March through June to begin their breeding activities. They body surf in on the tips of crashing waves, stranding themselves helplessly on the beaches, where they can be picked up by fishermen or predatory birds. Each female grunion wriggles and burrows her tail into the sand and begins frantically laying eggs while the males wriggle beside the females, depositing sperm into the sand beside them. That done, the grunions hop the next wave and return to the ocean (except for the unlucky ones who end up in frying pans or bird beaks). The eggs are safe under the sand and lie undisturbed while the tides are low. Warmed by the heat of the sun for fifteen days, they hatch and swim out to sea to begin the process again. The adult grunions return every fifteen days during the season until the cycle is complete.

A Mouthful of Eggs

The catfish that lives in American coastal waters lays exceptionally large eggs, up to three-quarters of an inch in diameter. After these eggs have been laid and fertilized the male catfish swims around collecting them in his mouth, where he can store up to forty-five eggs. The eggs remain there for six weeks before finally hatching.

The Mediterranean cardinal fish, whose eggs are much smaller than those of the American catfish, can hold up to 20,000 tiny eggs in its mouth.

The Cast of the Exploding Worm

As the moon waxes from a silver crescent into a swollen, incandescent globe over Fiji and Samoa each November, the tip of the palolo's body swells as it engorges itself with eggs or sperm. By some mysterious signal the little marine worms all emerge from their hiding places in the coral reefs on the night of the full moon. When all is ready the ends of their bodies simultaneously break off and burst like millions of exploding cigars, turning the ocean milky-white with sperm that immediately begins swimming energetically toward the free-floating eggs. This oceanic orgasm provides all the feeding creatures of the sea with a one-night protein pig-out, and they rush to feast on this delicious marine ambrosia. There is so much of it in the ocean that enough sperm and eggs escape the nocturnal harvest and unite to continue the existence of the little animal.

Piggyback Fish Eggs
The female bitterling deposits its eggs into the gill chambers of freshwater mussels, after which the male of this species of fish deposits its milt nearby. During the normal process of feeding, the mussel draws in the milt from the male bitterling and unwittingly fertilizes the eggs.

An Awesome Orgasm
The impressive exploding-tail trick of the palolo sea worm is confined to the area around Fiji and Samoa. The Woodstock of the South Pacific takes place each year in the Great Barrier Reef off the coast of Australia, a coral reef stretching over a thousand miles from the tip of Cape York Peninsula halfway down the eastern flank of that vast subcontinent.

One of the great natural wonders of the world, the reef was built entirely by a tiny sea animal called the coral polyp. Once affixed to the reef each polyp secretes a fluid that hardens into a protective shell, then spends the rest of its life inside the coral walls it has made. When it dies, succeeding generations of polyps build their homes atop the vacated shells. Entire islands rose from the seas over centuries, all made by the minuscule animal. In keeping with the little polyp's think-big philosophy, on the same hour of the same night of the year from time immemorial every polyp, on some unseen heavenly signal, releases sperm and eggs into the seas to be fertilized, producing more coral polyps to build yet more coral reefs. Scientists believe the massive, continentwide orgasm is related to the phases of the moon and the temperature of the sea. Exactly how it all happens over thousands of miles at the same time each year remains a tantalizing mystery.

Private Parts
The female snail's vagina is in her head.

The female octopus has her vagina in her nose. If the male octopus approaches the female when she is not ready for mating, the female octupus will bite off his penis (one of eight!) and swim away with it.

The female land tortoise, when ready for mating, will eat voraciously and gain so much weight that when she pulls her head inside her shell, her vagina pops out behind her, ready for mating.

Male snakes have two penises, both of which are completely internal until they are erect. They are actually two separate organs that work together during mating.

The penis of the blue whale is six to nine feet long.

Dolphins have voluntary erections. The dolphin has developed remarkably quick voluntary muscles that can retract the erect penis, protecting it from injury. Dolphins can mate at any time, like humans, and do it for fun and play. Whales, in contrast, mate only during their season.

ANIMALS CARING

It is crucial to the survival of each and every species that fertilized eggs are allowed to develop free from harm. One of an animal's most important activities involves caring for its developing young, thereby ensuring that its offspring get a good start in the world. Whether carefully hidden away from sight and scent or actively defended from predators, the next generation relies on much of their parents' time and energy for their survival.

Home Sweet Home

There are a few types of fish that construct nests for their offspring. The best known of these nest-builders are the sticklebacks. The male stickleback will construct a nest by binding together living seaweed fronds with the aid of threadlike secretions produced from its kidneys. Four inches in length and pear-shaped, these nests have a hole in the center created by the boring action of the head of the fish. Once the nest is completed, the eager male stickleback will perform elaborate courtship dances to lure a female into it to lay her eggs. Once the eggs are laid, the female vacates the nest and the male keeps guard over it, aerating the water around the eggs with vigorous movements of his pectoral fins. Any approaching fish are quickly driven away.

Siamese fighting fish are known for their aggressiveness. Their fights are a popular spectator sport in Thailand, where gamblers take odds on the underwater warriors. When ready to mate, the male begins blowing bubbles until he has a mass of them. Not one to waste time on formalities, he grabs the female, wraps his body around her, and squeezes the eggs out of her, fertilizing them as they emerge. The eggs are transferred to the bubble mass, which becomes their nest. The well-named fighting fish guards his nest ferociously and drives off any fish with the temerity to investigate, even those that are much larger than himself.

When the eggs of the Siamese fighting fish hatch, the newborn fry immediately set out to explore their world. The father is alarmed but would find it impossible to try to round up each of the small fry. Instead the father stays put and begins to tremble violently. Sensing danger, the young fry immediately head straight for their father for safety. As soon as they are within range the father scoops them into his mouth and spits them back into the nest. After several days of this, the young have grown to a size where they can begin to fend for themselves. At that point they swim deeper in the water and are out of range of the father fish's vibratory cautions.

Unusual Incubations

A tiny South American frog less than an inch long has a big mouth when it comes to tadpoles. A group of males congregates near several dozen eggs from a female until they are ready to hatch. The males then put from five to fifteen eggs in their vocal pouch with their tongues. Inside the frog's throat the eggs grow from tadpoles into little frogs; then they hop out to begin their frog careers.

The Australian stomach-brooding frog takes the process a step further. The female swallows the eggs and turns her stomach into a womb until the small fry are ready to emerge. During the gestation the frog stops using her stomach for digestion and even breathes through her skin when the bulk of the growing babies collapses her lungs. When ready, the bloated mother opens her mouth and, one by one, the froglets emerge and hop out. Sometimes a baby frog turns around and goes back for a while before emerging permanently. One mother frog is reported to have discharged twenty-six babies from the stomach incubator. No other animal incubates babies in this way.

A Safe Haven for Cod Fry
The cod is probably the most prolific of all fish. At one spawning a single female codfish may lay as many as eight million eggs. These millions of eggs will float to the surface of the sea and drift with the currents in masses of

plankton and seaweed. As the embryonic fish develops in its egg, developing a slender body with a pair of enormous eyes, tremendous numbers of them are consumed by plankton-eating animals. When the young fish that survive reach one inch in length they seek shelter under the umbrellas of the giant jellyfish. It is astonishing that the cod fry are able to avoid being stung and instantly killed by the jellyfish's tentacles, which are massed with deadly stinging cells. They find a safe haven there, since no fish will venture between the stinging tentacles to catch them.

The Male Midwife
The male midwife toad is called the bell toad for his loud, bell-like cry. The female lays a string of eggs, three to four feet long, which the two-inch male struggles to wrap around his body like a huge sash. For over a month he lugs this load about, hiding during the day and dragging himself to the stream at night to moisten the eggs. When they finally hatch, the exhausted father gratefully watches the tiny tadpoles swim away. He remains silent for the rest of the year, possibly from fatigue, resuming his famous cry the following spring.

Feathered Baby-sitters
The American cowbird lays its eggs in the nests of other birds. They are hatched and cared for by the original nest-builder, who is either broad-minded or can't tell the difference. This is an anachronism from the past when bison herds roamed the great plains attended by flocks of cowbirds, who found their food supply on the backs of the bison in the form of blood-sucking ticks. Because the herds were always on the move there was never enough time for cowbirds to build a proper nest—if they did, they would find their food supply had moved away. The great

wandering herds foraging hundreds of miles in all directions are gone forever, but the cowbird remains, confining its attentions nowadays to cows and other sedentary barnyard denizens. It still lays its eggs in other birds' nests, although the reason for this no longer exists.

Huddle-of-the-Year Award

After feeding in the sea, the emperor penguins inhabiting the freezing Antarctic region must trek as far as 60 miles to their rookeries, which are well back from the areas where the ice meets the ocean.

Incubation of the eggs is shared by the male and female penguins. The male takes first shift while the female returns to the sea to feed after laying her eggs. She may be away for as long as three weeks, and the male may well have fasted for as long as forty days before his mate returns to take her turn keeping the eggs warm in the 40-below-zero temperatures.

The emperor penguin makes no nest, since it would be impossible to keep the eggs warm if they were deposited in the ice and there are no materials available to make a nest that might raise the egg above it. Instead the male penguin stands in an upright position and balances the eggs on top of his feet, where they are covered from above by a fold of abdominal skin and held against the warm vascular blood patches of the abdomen. Although the ambient air temperature may be as low as minus 40 degrees centigrade, the temperature inside the incubating egg remains at a comfortable 31 degrees centigrade.

During the six weeks of incubation the male penguins remains virtually immobile, and he eats no food because none is available. Even a few seconds of exposure to the freezing air would kill the eggs. In order to avoid freezing to death the incubating male emperors huddle together in groups of up to six thousand, those on the outside of the huddle periodically pushing towards the middle to be replaced by others so that none remain exposed to the outside for very long.

Over the Cuckoo's Nest

The cuckoo bird has a habit of laying its eggs in the nests of other bird species and then dropping the eggs of the host bird over the rim of the nest so that the cuckoo young, when hatched, get all of the food meant for the original offspring.

Worth Her Weight in Eggs

The female salmon releases an average of 900 eggs for each pound of her body weight, a twenty-pound salmon releasing an estimated 18,000 eggs. These eggs are laid in hollows excavated by the salmon's skillful sweeping of stones with its tail. As soon as the eggs are fertilized by the males, the females cover the nests by sweeping gravel over them. Not all of the eggs are fertilized. Of those that are, few make it to hatching, and once hatched the fingerlings are easy prey for predators. Adult salmon are hunted relentlessly by other fish and by man, reducing their odds of survival even further. Because of the large numbers of eggs each salmon produces, the species continues to survive against the odds.

Waiting for Baby Bird	Incubation Period (days)
Finch	12
Wren	16
Falcon	28
Swan	30
Ostrich	42
Hawk	44
Emperor penguin	63
Royal albatross	79

Hatching By the Heat of the Sand

During breeding season vast numbers of common marine turtles leave the open sea and approach the sandy beaches of tropical and subtropical coasts. On a bright moonlit night the females come ashore by the thousands, having previously mated in the sea. Once on land each female turtle proceeds to form a hole in the warm sand by using her hind flippers. The sand is ladled out alternately with each flipper, accumulating behind the turtle, until after about ten minutes the hole is 18 to 24 inches deep. Over the next twenty minutes or so up to 200 eggs are dropped one by one into the hole. The industrious turtle mother then scrapes back the loose sand over her eggs and levels and smooths the surface so well that no sign is left of the disturbance. Once her task is completed the turtle returns to the sea, leaving her eggs to hatch by the heat of the sand.

A Thermometer in the Mouth

The only group of birds who do not sit on their eggs to incubate them are the megapodes or "incubator birds." The heat needed to incubate their eggs is obtained by rotting vegetation collected into large mounds that serve as artificial incubators.

The nesting mounds of these Australian birds are extremely large. For several weeks in early spring the birds collect what would amount to cart-loads of organic materials by grasping a quantity in their feet and throwing it backwards towards a common center. No leaf or blade of

grass remains unused on the surface of the ground for a considerable distance from the mound. After these mounds become saturated with rain, the megapodes will cover the whole pile with sand so that the rotting process can begin. When the temperature within the mound reaches 92 degrees Fahrenheit, as measured with incredible accuracy by a beakful of sand, the female megapodes are ready to lay their first eggs. The eggs are carefully deposited in a circle within the mound, an arm's length down. The females will lay as many as thirty eggs in a season, representing a total egg weight of three times their own body weight.

The megapodes will adjust the temperature of the mound if the weather is chilly or windy by placing more sand on it. If the internal mound temperature rises even one degree past 92 degrees Fahrenheit, the male birds will assist the females in removing sand to cool down the mound.

Prenatal Communication

Quail eggs talk to each other. Inside each egg the unborn chick struggles in the confined space, clicking its beak against the shell and chirping weakly. Chicks inside neighboring eggs hear the sounds of their siblings-to-be. They can synchronize the hour of hatching so all come out into the world at approximately the same time. If they were not all born together, the hen would be faced with the problem of caring for the eggs still unhatched and simultaneously getting food for the hungry newborn chicks. As they wait to be born, the chicks listen to the sounds their mother makes and so become accustomed to her voice. This helps them identify her after birth. When the mother hen cries in alarm, the chicks inside the unhatched egg know danger is near and fall silent until, through the eggshell, they hear her reassuring sounds again.

Badger Parents

The solitary badger doesn't even like other badgers, usually picking a fight when they encounter another of their species. Their mating is casual and often accidental, after which the male and female go their separate ways, never to meet again. The impregnated female will not even begin to develop an embryo until months after the encounter, a trait shared with others of the weasel family. When young badgers are born they nurse for a few weeks, after which they go out on foraging trips for instruction by the mother. A few weeks of that are more than the mother can stand. She soon kicks the youngsters out to fend for themselves and nevermore be seen. Perhaps this traumatic childhood accounts for the badger's surly disposition.

Spiders on the Wind

Newborn spiders, in search of uncrowded territory for their voracious appetites, have developed a nifty and highly effective means of traveling over vast distances: they hitch a ride with the wind. The tiny spider climbs as high as it can on an exposed grass stem, turns its face to the wind, raises its abdomen in the air, and secretes a gossamer silk thread that is drawn out by the breeze into an incredibly thin line. When this "parachute" or "balloon" thread is several feet long it achieves sufficient buoyancy to lift the nearly weightless spider from its anchorage and carry it into the air. Small spiderlings can be carried many miles on their gossamer threads. In Charles Darwin's famous account of his voyages, he describes several thousand baby spiders coming aboard ship on November 1, 1832, when the ship was *sixty miles* from the nearest land!

Committed Parents

The ocean-loving albatross has one of the longest incubation periods of any egg-laying animal—up to 70 days. Both parents take turns sitting on the nest during incubation. The albatross lays a single egg, and when hatched the baby will remain in the nest for eleven months. The parent birds will stray many miles from the nest in search of food for their offspring.

Sperm Whales

The female sperm whale, averaging 32 feet in length, can contain a calf nearly half its size and weighing more than 17,000 pounds. The water in which the whale lives helps to support the enormous weight of the developing fetal whale. After the baby whales are born, special muscles at the mother's nipples will pump milk down the young whale's throat. This method is necessary because whales cannot purse their lips and suckle.

Dramatic Weight Gains

At birth a blue whale is already 20 to 24 feet long and is the fastest-growing animal on earth, increasing by as much as 200 pounds per day (8 pounds per hour!). By the end of seven months the calf measures over 50 feet in length, and after two years it is 70 to 75 feet long and sexually mature.

Fish without Eggs

The female coelacanth incubates its eggs in its genital tract and gives birth to live young. This same method of reproduction occurs in guppies and mollies, as well as all members of the surfperch family. The tiger shark gives birth to as many as 60 pups at a time, each about two feet long. While retained in the oviducts of the mother shark, the eggs are supplied with nutritive fluid from special filaments projecting from the oviduct walls. The vast majority of fishes, however, lay eggs that develop outside of the body.

Special Deliveries
The North American meadow mouse produces up to seventeen litters per year, the greatest number of litters of any mammal. The armadillo usually gives birth to four genetically identical infants of the same sex.

Gestation Periods in the Animal Kingdom
In general, the larger the mammal, the longer it carries its young in the womb. The following list presents the average length of gestation for a variety of mammals.

Animal	Gestation Period (days)
Elephant	625
Rhinoceros	560
Giraffe	410
Camel	406
Whale	365
Horse	340
Cow	280
Human	266
Hippopotamus	240
Chimpanzee	237
Goat	151
Leopard	105
Dog	63
Cat	60
Rabbit	30
Mouse	19
Hamster	16

Elephant Midwives

A female elephant usually will give birth to her first calf when she is sixteen years of age, and will continue to breed until she reaches the age of eighty. An extraordinary event, often observed on the savannahs of Africa and even in the jungles of Asia by rangers and scientists, is the birth of a baby elephant. After a gestation period of about 22 months the mother elephant is tightly surrounded and protected by a ring of other female elephants. As the mother's 4-to-6-minute contractions begin, one or two of the attending females will take a position at her birth canal to carefully guide the newborn out and remove the baby from the fetal membrane.

After the delivery of the 235-to 250-pound, 38-to-40-inch-long baby elephant, the elephant midwives or aunties, as they are often called by scientists, will carefully remove the amniotic sac and toss it into the air so that it will land as a sterile sheet on which to stand the newborn elephant. Meanwhile the male elephants present in the herd at the birth scene will drive away any approaching vultures or other animals.

The midwife elephants collected around the newborn will carefully bring it to its feet using their trunks and legs. The rest of the herd will wait for two or three days after the birth until the newborn is ready to move on with the others. Elephants give birth to only one baby at a time, except in extremely rare cases in which twins are born.

After giving birth the mother stands over her baby, touching it constantly with her tongue, and will even lift it gently to support it on its new legs.